PEARL HARBOR

PEARL HARBOR

A VISUAL HISTORY COMMEMORATING THE DATE THAT WILL LIVE IN INFAMY

RANDY ROBERTS AND DAVID WELKY

becker&mayer!
BOOK PRODUCERS

TO ALL THOSE WHO SERVED.

ISBN-13: 978-1-60380-388-5

Pearl Harbor: A Visual History Commemorating the Date that Will Live in Infamy is produced by becker&mayer!,
Bellevue, Washington.

becker&mayer!
BOOK PRODUCERS
Produced by becker&mayer!, LLC.
11120 NE 33rd Place, Suite 101
Bellevue, WA 98004
www.beckermayer.com

Design by Rosebud Eustace
Editorial by Kirsten Colton
Photo research by Farley Bookout
Production coordination by Olivia Holmes

10   9   8   7   6   5   4   3   2   1

Manufactured in China

TABLE OF CONTENTS

PROLOGUE
IF I ONLY HAD A GUN IN MY HANDS

It was supposed to be a junket to paradise. That's how Americans regarded the territory of Hawaii before December 7, 1941—a land of swaying palm trees, towering emerald mountains, brightly colored birds, and cobalt blue seas, of Polynesian beauties, luaus, and an escape from mainland worries. In early December 1941, when the San Jose State College and Willamette University football teams sailed to Honolulu to play against the University of Hawaii to support the Shriners Hospitals for Children, the players considered it a once-in-a-lifetime trip. It would be one of those college adventures that would remain with them the rest of their lives.

Few of the players thought much about world affairs. Certainly they realized relations between the United States and Japan were rocky. And when they arrived in Hawaii, one member of the Willamette contingent recalled that he heard talk that war

LEFT | Hawaii—the name itself was exotic, conjuring images of swaying palm trees nestled against the blue Pacific Ocean. In the early age of long-distance commercial flight, it was a dream destination.

7

"was inevitable," though most everyone felt "the Hawaiian Islands would remain out of the area of battle at least in the opening stages of the hostilities. Japan would not dare attack an island as heavily fortified as theirs," he recalled. Yet on the whole, players engaged in more conversation with the islanders about "King Football" than about the prospects of war. After all, Hawaii was a veritable Shangri-la, a retreat from the nasty affairs of nations.

Willamette played their game against Hawaii on December 6, losing a hard-fought contest 20 to 6. But it hardly mattered, for on the next day the American players were scheduled for a daylong tour of Oahu,

ABOVE | For the American military, Honolulu *was* Pearl Harbor, the home of the Pacific Fleet, close enough to Japan to exert US power but far enough away to be safe. Safety, however, was an illusion.

accompanied by coeds from the local university. About 8:00 a.m., most of the players were just beginning to rouse out of their beds when they heard something unusual. It sounded like sharp but muffled explosions. Just some routine army and navy maneuvers, they suspected.

San Jose State coach Ben Winkelman, his hair cut short and his face red from the sun, was eating breakfast in the dining room of the Moana Hotel on Waikiki. As a waiter was pouring him another glass of papaya juice, out in the bay Winkelman saw what looked like a large geyser. It was as if God had dropped an enormous lead football into the Pacific.

"They must be having practice this morning," he told the waiter, assuming the navy was taking target practice.

Without much of a glance, the waiter answered, "Oh, no, that is a whale, or shark, or some big fish. They play around out there all the time."

But as more geysers spit into the air, accompanied by concussions of sound, Winkelman concluded that "the whales were not that playful." Probably maneuvers, he thought, as he sipped his juice.

George Constable, a tackle on the Willamette team, thought the same thing. He watched "the pretty realistic maneuvers" from the roof of the Moana. "We heard shells, saw splashes, but were kind of oblivious," he wrote. "Ironically, I had a Kodak box camera in my room, but I wasn't about to go get it just to take snapshots of practice runs."

By 8:30 a.m. the reality that the war had commenced had set in. Out in the bay, and over toward Pearl Harbor, there was utter confusion. Winkelman and the other diners watched as naval vessels circled back and forth, shooting volleys of antiaircraft fire into the air. They witnessed planes diving toward ships and bombs exploding in the water. Closer to Waikiki, several blasts sounded nearby. Within blocks of the Moana a "fragmentary shell" left a crater in the street, thousands of holes in a newly constructed stucco building, and sheared off ornamental trees.

Anger pervaded the confusion. Chet Carsten of Camino, California, vented both. "Gosh," he told Coach Winkelman, "I feel helpless. If I only had a gun in my hands, I'd feel better."

CHAPTER 1
REHEARSAL FOR PEARL HARBOR

The road to Pearl Harbor began a decade before December 7, 1941, when Japan began to reject democracy and liberalism.

The signs of the violence and militarism to come were clear on November 14, 1930 when a right-wing, ultra-nationalist assassin shot Prime Minister Hamaguchi Osachi in a Tokyo railway station. Hamaguchi was the quintessential Japanese liberal. A member of the Constitutional Democratic Party, he supported women's suffrage, fiscal austerity, and limiting the influence of the military. While in office he even pushed through the ratification of the London Naval Conference, which curtailed spending by limiting the number of naval cruisers from Japan, the United States, and Britain. Looking to the democratic West for ideas, dressing like a well-heeled London banker, Hamaguchi embodied the economic and political traits that had gained force in Japan during the 1920s.

But the winds of the Great Depression chilled the liberal landscape. The worldwide economic crisis caused the Japanese to suffer terribly, and Hamaguchi's deflationary economic policies—including returning to the gold standard—sent the country into a tailspin. Exports declined by 50 percent in two years; silk prices dropped 65 percent in one year. The rural population was

LEFT | With the onset of the Great Depression, many Japanese military and political leaders turned away from liberalism and reform and toward militarism and conquest. In 1931, Manchuria became the target of Japanese aggression.

disproportionately impacted. To survive, some peasants ate the bark off trees while others sold their daughters to city brothels. Since many of the junior army officers came from rural backgrounds, the peasants' suffering did not go unnoticed. Japan's problems, these officers felt, resulted from their nation's entanglement with the ideas and institutions of the West. Liberalism was the cause of the country's ills, not the solution, they thought.

Many junior officers joined such secret organizations as the Black Dragon Society, which used assassination to undermine Japanese liberalism. Hamaguchi was shot by such a fanatic. Though he survived the attack, it contributed to his early death. His successor as prime minister was also assassinated, as were other liberal reformers. Soon

"government by assassination" had replaced liberal democracy, and the military increasingly exerted its power.

The answer to Japan's troubles, according to conservative military leaders, was independence through expansion. In the previous eighty years, the population of Japan had doubled, and the nation's rapid industrialization strained its limited pool of natural resources. In the mid-1930s it imported two-thirds of its oil from the United States and all of its rubber and tin from the European colonies in Southeast Asia. Like Adolf Hitler and his followers in Germany, conservatives in Japan cried out for more territory with a tone that smacked of manifest destiny. Why should the Western powers control the raw materials of Asia? Why shouldn't Japan have more influence in its own region? Such questions led inevitably to talk of expansion and conquest. Tokyo had already annexed Formosa (Taiwan) in 1895, and Korea fifteen years later. But the military and its civilian supporters had still grander ideas. The ores of Manchuria, rubber of Indochina and Malaya, and oil of the Dutch East Indies beckoned. With unlimited access to the resources that were close by, Japanese industry might rival that of the United States.

Japanese expansion was powered by a unique engine. Instead of being dictated

ABOVE | The shooting of liberal Prime Minister Hamaguchi Osachi signaled the violent mood of Japan in the early 1930s. He died soon after the assassination attempt; liberalism in Japan did not last much longer.

from above, action was initiated from below. Dedicated, nationalistic midlevel staff officers often took grave matters of state into their own hands. Imbued with the spirit of *gekokujo*—a sort of "loyal insubordination"—they justified unauthorized actions to achieve some higher good. That higher good might be the assassination of a liberal politician, or overseas conquest to end their country's economic ills. Any aggression, any heinous act, could be rationalized as a defense of the state.

In 1931, a cabal of officers in Japan's Kwantung Army in Manchuria resolved to force a change in government policy. It began when the Tokyo government, facing increased violence against politicians and a swooning economy, decided to curb the army's activities. In September it sent a senior general with a message ordering the army to practice "prudence and patience" in all relations with China in Manchuria. Hoping to derail the intentions of their political leaders, junior staff officers who had learned about

ABOVE | The Kwantung Army was Japan's military arm in Manchuria. Disciplined and often fanatical, it powered Japan's imperialistic drive.

the order sent a secret cable to associates in the Kwantung Army.

Their response was swift. On September 18, Japanese officers set off a series of explosions on a stretch of the main trunk of the South Manchurian Railway outside of Mukden, in China to the west of Korea. In the noise and confusion that followed, there were minor skirmishes between Japanese and Chinese troops. Then a senior Japanese officer ordered a full-scale attack on a Chinese barracks and the capture of the walled city of Mukden. Soon Japan had extended its control over all of Manchuria.

The "Mukden Incident" elicited howls of protest. Chinese and Americans requested that the League of Nations take steps to end the fighting, and even a Japanese consul on the scene attempted to rein in the army—that

is, until one of the officers drew his sword in a threatening manner. The crisis was dropped squarely on the table of the government in Tokyo. Should it disavow the action and demand that the Kwantung Army behave peacefully? Doing so would admit that the government lacked control over its own military forces and entail a significant loss of face. Or should the government accept the action as a fait accompli and increase its position in Manchuria?

After several ambiguous statements, Tokyo took the latter course. Republic of China leader Chiang Kai-shek was in no position militarily to oppose the Japanese in Manchuria due to internal revolts in his country. Instead, he ordered his forces back behind the Great Wall. In an obvious attempt to disguise its naked aggression, Japan then established a quasi-independent government in Manchuria by convincing Henry Puyi, the last of the Manchu emperors of China, to lead the newly christened Manchukuo ("land of the Manchus"). Of course, Puyi was a puppet. Any decision of real importance was made in Japan. Puyi might have signed new laws, but they had been written in Tokyo.

The world's response to Japan's land grab was at best tepid. Russia was too embroiled in its own domestic problems to do anything,

ABOVE | Henry Puyi, the last of China's Manchu emperors, was installed by the Japanese as the ruler of the new state of Manchukuo. But Japan retained real authority.

ABOVE | Japanese soldiers proudly display a skull and crossbones flag in occupied Manchuria (Manchukuo).
The country remained under their thumb until the end of World War II.

and China did little more than protest. Almost a year after the Manchurian Incident, as it was also called, the League of Nations formed a commission to investigate the affair. It concluded that the incident and the establishment of Manchukuo did not represent the will of the inhabitants, hardly news to anyone in the West who had followed the situation. In response, in September 1932 the League condemned Japan's actions and called on it to withdraw from Manchuria, though it issued no sanctions.

Yosuke Matsuoka, Japan's leading delegate to the League, answered the charges by insisting that his nation would "oppose any attempt at international control of Manchuria." He asked, "Would the American people agree to such control of the Panama Canal Zone; would the British permit it over Egypt?" The answer was obvious, he thought. After concluding his speech, he walked out

of the session. Hisses mingled with applause in the galleries as he led the black-clad Japanese delegation out of the assembly. "We are not coming back," he said.

The Manchurian Incident was a dress rehearsal for other acts of aggression during the 1930s. The world community might condemn the actions of Japan, Italy, and Germany, but words were weak responses to armed force. The world community had more pressing matters with which to contend. In the West, the Depression and the preservation of international peace trumped the fate of Manchuria—or Ethiopia, Spain, the Sudetenland, or even Austria. The placating of a dictator's aggressive, expansionist actions, which would become known as "appeasement," appeared in Asia several years before Hitler assumed power in Germany.

The Manchurian Incident also helped to undercut civilian control of Japan and increased the influence of the military, especially the firebrand element. The future belonged to those midlevel officers of action. For them Manchuria became a training ground. There, beyond the eyes of prying civilians and public officials, they trained and held large-scale maneuvers. During the next five years, the Kwantung Army grew larger, bolder, and better skilled, preparing to advance from Manchuria into China.

ABOVE | Victor Bulwer-Lytton, the Earl of Lytton, led a League of Nations fact-finding commission to ascertain responsibility for the conflict between Japan and China in Manchuria.

Talk of war, and planning for it, strangled the liberal forces of international cooperation and democratic reform in Japan. In the 1930s the Japanese economy began to convert to wartime austerity, encouraging government monopolies, prohibiting exports considered necessary to the military, and banning luxury goods. The government imprisoned leftists and pacifists, and cracked down on labor unions at the same time as it encouraged shows of patriotism and martial prowess. Slowly, and as yet unconsciously, Japan was moving down a path that would lead to Pearl Harbor.

In the military itself the *bushido* spirit—or "way of the warrior"—gained prominence. It emphasized fighting to the death for the empire. In warfare there were only two honorable results: victory or death. Surrender

ABOVE | The fanaticism that led to Japanese *kamikaze* attacks in the later stages of World War II were part of the nation's *bushido* code. Death was preferable to dishonor.

ABOVE | A magazine cover pictured a kamikaze pilot preparing to take his last flight. Service to his nation was his highest goal.

was deemed cowardly, an affront to the revered emperor. In fact, in Japanese military regulations no soldiers and sailors were to be taken prisoner by the enemy; they were to die first, by their own hands if necessary. In the war ahead, the code would sanction rash *banzai* attacks into fortified positions, one-way *kamikaze* assaults onto the decks of enemy ships, and *seppuku*—"stomach cutting"—by leaders who were faced with failure. It is hardly surprising that Japan's state-produced World War II films always ended with the death of most, if not all, of the main characters.

The *bushido* spirit also led to a reckless arrogance and icy disregard for the enemy. Military leaders believed their soldiers and sailors—indeed, their entire culture—were superior to those of other nations. Japan's army might be small, its weapons inferior, and its logistics primitive, but, its commanders maintained, its spirit alone guaranteed victory. Far from being apprehensive about or wary of war, the nation's leaders seemed to welcome it as an opportunity to display their superiority. Bellicosely nationalistic, undeniably expansionist, and culturally arrogant, it was only a matter of time until Japan stumbled into another conflict.

China was the mostly likely trouble spot. Japanese and Chinese troops brushed against each other in northern China, and as a result of a 1901 agreement, Japanese troops were entitled to maneuver in specific areas in and

ABOVE | After the incident on the Marco Polo Bridge, full-scale warfare erupted between Japan and China. The bolt-action Type 38 rifle was a staple in the Japanese arsenal.

around Peking. On the night of July 7, 1937, about ten miles west of Peking on the banks of the Yongding River, an incident occurred. A company of Japanese troops encamped near the beautiful, centuries-old "Marco Polo Bridge" (Lugouquia) across the river from the strategically important walled town of Wanping. The troops were authorized to fire blanks into the air to simulate the sounds of battle, and undoubtedly they did. Then at 10:30 p.m. the Chinese garrison on the other side of the Yongding apparently fired several live shells toward the Japanese position. (There is some controversy about who fired the shells.) There were no casualties, but a roll call revealed that one Japanese soldier was missing. His commander assumed that the Chinese had taken the man prisoner.

A Japanese officer insisted that the Chinese soldiers permit his troops to cross the bridge and enter Wanping to look for the soldier and investigate the cause of the shelling. The Chinese refused. Although the missing soldier soon rejoined his unit, the Japanese forces were spoiling for action. They attacked the bridge, but were repulsed after a spirited engagement. It was a small affair, really, hardly worthy of notice, but several historians would later call it the first battle of World War II.

During the next few days the two sides continued to skirmish. At stake was a railway bridge that straddled the river near the Marco Polo Bridge and a crucial junction

that controlled rail access to the cities of Tianjin, Kalgan, and Taiyuan. The actions produced negligible results. But in Nanking, Chiang Kai-shek's walled capital, and Tokyo political battle lines were hardening. On July 8, Chiang wrote in his diary, "The time has come to make the decision to fight." "If we allow one more inch of our territory to be lost," he announced, "we shall be guilty of an unpardonable crime against our race." Recently installed Japanese prime minister Prince Fumimaro Konoe was equally intransigent, claiming that his nation was "forced to resort to resolute action to bring sense to the Nanking government." Instead of taking the small steps necessary to avoid war, both leaders took giant leaps into the fray, sending more troops to the hot spots.

Without a firm declaration of hostilities, the Sino-Japanese War intensified. Because Chiang's finest divisions, trained and equipped by Germans, were garrisoned near Shanghai, he launched his assault there, gambling that he could force Japan away

ABOVE | The storming of Nanking began with an explosion at the main gate, opening the walled city to Japanese armor and infantry forces. Many of the Chinese soldiers inside the walls had lost the will to fight.

from the northern front. Chiang's campaign was a complete debacle. Although the Chinese inflicted some 40,000 casualties, they suffered as many as 250,000. By mid-November they were streaming westward in an unorganized retreat, scrambling toward Nanking. The Japanese followed in hot pursuit.

China's defense of Nanking suffered from poor strategy and demoralized troops. Many soldiers were more interested in shedding their uniforms, putting on civilian clothes, and looting their fellow countrymen than in confronting the enemy. On December 13 Japanese forces broke through the city's gates and unleashed a seven-week reign of terror on the people inside of the walls. History remembers the period as the "Rape of

Nanking," and for sheer brutality, violence, and inhumanity, it was one of the worst episodes in all of World War II. In her history of the event, Iris Chang wrote, "The chronicle of humankind's cruelty to fellow humans is a long and sorry tale. But if it is true that even in such horror tales there are degrees of ruthlessness, then few atrocities in world history compare in intensity and scale to the Rape of Nanking during World War II."

The atrocities began with the killing of prisoners. One Japanese battalion received the order: "ALL PRISONERS OF WAR ARE TO BE EXECUTED." And the Japanese carried out the order with ruthless efficiency. Their strategy was to offer fair treatment to any soldier who surrendered, then tie up those who

ABOVE | Japanese troops tortured, mutilated, and killed hundreds of thousands of Chinese soldiers and civilians. They dumped many of the dead outside the city's walls or into the Yangtze River.

accepted the offer, separate them into smaller groups, and finally kill them. Japanese soldiers were amazed that tens of thousands of Chinese troops—a larger force, in fact, than Japan's—were willing to surrender, an act they considered cowardice. Dehumanizing the POWs, one Japanese commander later wrote, "They all walked in droves, like ants crawling on the ground. They looked like a bunch of homeless people, with ignorant expressions on their faces."

Soon the killing commenced. At a spot near Mufu Mountain the Japanese executed an estimated fifty-seven thousand military and civilian prisoners. Disposing of the bodies proved more daunting than the executions. There were not enough ditches to contain the corpses nor enough fuel to burn

them, so most were dumped into the Yangtze River, which ran red with blood.

Mass executions of civilians followed the killing of soldiers. The Japanese moved house to house, massacring the inhabitants and tossing their bodies outside the city walls. Bored with simply shooting or bayoneting their victims, Japanese soldiers engaged in sadistic killing games. They held contests to see who could behead their victims the fastest. One witness recalled that the Japanese troops laughed during such contests, some yelling, "Kill and count! Count and kill!" He recalled, "There was no sign of remorse at all."

Other prisoners were tortured to death. Japanese soldiers buried them alive, mutilated their bodies, threw them naked into

ABOVE | Skeletal remains of the Rape of Nanking are visible in a mass grave at the Memorial Hall of the Victims of the Nanking Massacre by Japanese Invaders, which details the extent of the atrocities.

icy rivers, or buried them to their waists and watched as German shepherds tore them apart. They impaled babies, saturated victims with acid, and hung people by their tongues. They practiced inhumanity on a universal scale.

One expert on the subject claimed that Nanking witnessed the second worst outbreak of rape during a war in history. There are no precise figures for the number of women raped, but the estimates range from a low of twenty thousand to a high of eighty thousand. Many of the women were killed after repeated rapes, while others lived with the painful memories and psychological trauma of their ordeals. Nor were all the victims female. Chinese men and boys were also sodomized.

How many Chinese did the Japanese kill during the six weeks of horror? Again there is no exact number. Officials at the Memorial Hall of the Victims of the Nanking Massacre by Japanese Invaders use the round number of 300,000. Other estimates run as high as 430,000 and as low as 200,000. But it is impossible to measure barbarity or to put a number on inhumanity. A Japanese official sent in January 1938 to China to investigate the slaughter wrote, "[The] Japanese Army behaved and [is] continuing [to] behave in [a] manner reminiscent [of] Attila [and] his

Huns. [Not] less than three hundred thousand Chinese civilians slaughtered, in many cases [in] cold blood."

Japan's bloody march from Shanghai to Nanking sent ripples of concern through foreign nationals living in China. Shanghai was the economic hub of the country, and during the battle for the city thousands of civilians were killed and wounded. As Japan's troops approached the walls of Nanking, US authorities began to evacuate American diplomatic, missionary, and business personnel from Chiang's capital. The mission led to a direct—and deadly—confrontation between the United States and Japan. Just as they would at Pearl Harbor, Japan demonstrated a willingness to attack American sailors without warning.

In 1858 the United States, along with Great Britain, France, and Russia, had won treaty rights to patrol Chinese rivers and territorial waters. By 1937, eight American gunboats, a proud little squadron of stubby, top-heavy, flat-bottomed ships, steamed along the lower Yangtze River. Their mission was inscribed on a bronze plaque on the USS *Panay*: "For the protection of American life and property in the Yangtze River Valley and

its tributaries, and the furtherance of American good will in China."

Service aboard a gunboat in the Yangtze Patrol was about as good as it got in the navy. The *Panay* was built for four officers, forty-nine enlisted men, and about a dozen native crewmen. The commanding officers led *pukka* lives: Chinese servants looked after their every need; they were welcome in the most exclusive Shanghai clubs and tennis courts; and, if they desired, their wives traveled with them. Their men enjoyed outstanding food and cushy service, and a first-class seaman's pay of fifty-four dollars a month went a long way in the harbor saloons of Old China. Morale, therefore, was high. Problem sailors were soon shipped out to less

desirable places—and no right-minded seaman wanted that.

When the war between Japan and China spread upriver to Nanking, the *Panay* chugged into action. But it did so cautiously. Lieutenant Commander James Joseph Hughes, Annapolis trained and excellent at his job, curtailed all shore liberty and ordered two five-foot-by-nine-foot American flags lashed to the awnings of his ship's decks. He also flew the "Sunday Flag," a six-foot-by-eleven-foot ensign. At night, spotlights illuminated all the flags, which could be seen clearly from ashore and aloft. The flags as much as said: property of the United States, a neutral nation. And the *Panay* seemed such a sanctuary that Chinese vessels crowded near her during air raids.

ABOVE | The USS *Panay* was a flat-bottomed ship designed for river patrol. Though it was heavy and squat, service on the ship was a highly desired naval assignment.

The illusion of safety ended on Sunday, December 12, 1937. In the morning, a Japanese lieutenant and six soldiers with fixed bayonets boarded the gunboat. They wanted information about the location of Chinese soldiers. Commander Hughes refused to answer, claiming that as a neutral presence, the United States was friends with both nations and not part of the military operations of either. The Japanese lieutenant also tried to force Hughes to come ashore with him. Hughes refused.

A few hours later, while the *Panay* was anchored near several Standard Oil tankers, Japanese bombers swooped out of the sky and attacked, the red suns on their wingtips clearly visible. Several bombs exploded on the *Panay*'s decks, injuring scores of sailors, including Commander Hughes. Dive-bombers followed, spraying bullets at sailors scurrying close to the large American flags.

As the *Panay* sunk and the men on board abandoned ship, the Japanese pilots continued to attack, taking shots at survivors. Three people aboard the ship were killed (or soon died of their wounds), and forty-three sailors and five civilians were injured. The Standard Oil tankers were also destroyed, claiming the lives of or injuring more innocent American victims.

US ambassador to Japan Joseph Grew worried about the American reaction.

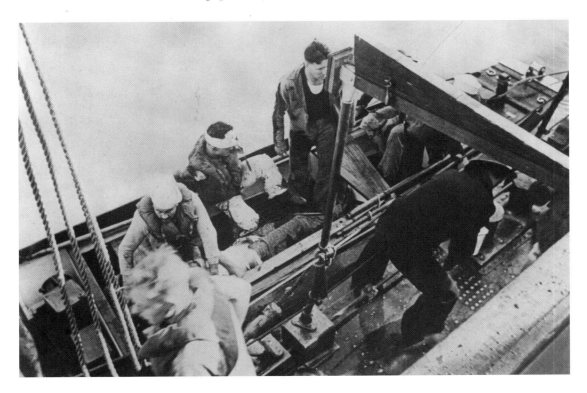

ABOVE | On Sunday, December 12, 1937, Japanese planes attacked and sank the *Panay*, killing several sailors and injuring scores. The sudden, unprovoked assault was a prelude to Pearl Harbor.

Japanese pilots had bombed an American ship, flying the Stars and Stripes. Grew still "remembered" the sinking of the *Maine*, which led directly to the Spanish-American War, and he feared that the sinking of the *Panay* might become another of those incendiary incidents that tipped public opinion toward war.

The American people deplored the Japanese behavior, but there was no desire for war in either public or government circles. It was an unfortunate event, yet not dramatic or meaningful enough to precipitate a declaration of war. "If a bright spot is to be discerned in so dark a picture, it has undoubtedly been furnished by the poise of the American people," editorialized the *Christian Century*. "Serious as the incident is viewed in this country, there has hardly been the slightest trace of such frenzied excitement as followed the sinking of the *Maine* and of the *Lusitania*. Comment in Congress has been notable in its restraint." Striking a noninterventionist tone, the editorial continued, "Shocked as the American public has been by the sinking of a naval vessel flying the American flag, an encouraging segment of opinion has raised the question: what was the gunboat doing in the midst of the war zone? . . . As the *Panay* affair is studied, we expect that this public demand for official extrication from the war peril will be increased. . . . The presence of American warships and of American troops where fighting is going on or where a military occupation is in progress is a constant tempting of fate."

Undoubtedly an anti-Western Japanese officer had ordered the bombing of the *Panay*, but in the days after the event Japan moved to still the choppy diplomatic waters. On Christmas Eve in Washington, Japanese officials made a complete apology. They accepted fault, but argued that the event was a tragic mistake. Because of a communications failure Japanese forces had lost track of the gunboat, and "dense smoke" along the Yangtze had made it impossible for the pilots to see the American flags. But, the officials said, those responsible for the event had been punished. The Japanese also cut a compensation check for $2,214,007.36. It was deemed "payment in full" for sinking the three Standard Oil tankers, the *Panay*, and the resultant deaths and injuries.

Officially the book was closed on the sinking of the *Panay*. But it was not forgotten. Twelve survivors of the gunboat were at Pearl Harbor on December 7, 1941. Once again they saw the bombers with red suns on their wings dive at American ships. This time the Japanese would pay a much higher price.

LOOK

ROOSEVELT, CHURCHILL and HITLER
by Dorothy Thompson

1-14-41

NORTH AMERICA

SOUTH AMERICA

PRESIDENT ROOSEVELT

WHAT WILL HAPPEN TO CONSCIENTIOUS OBJECTORS?

January 14, 1941 . . . 10¢

6d

CHAPTER 2
THE OTHER ENEMY

After the end of World War II, Congress investigated how and why the US government and military had failed to anticipate the Japanese attack on Pearl Harbor and were so totally unprepared against the air assault. As the Commander in Chief, US Pacific Fleet, (CinCPAC) at the time of the attack, Admiral Husband Kimmel was given by the committee the opportunity to defend himself, and he read a 108-page statement. His remarks answered many questions but by no means all of them. But its careful preparation and forceful logic said much about Kimmel's competency. And it left no doubt that he was a Navy Man through and through.

Every cadet who attends the US Naval Academy at Annapolis or the US Military Academy at West Point picks up a nickname. The lucky ones lose it sometime after graduation. Husband Edward "Hubby" Kimmel was one of the fortunate few whose moniker did not survive long after graduation. In fact, most of his life had seemed charmed. After graduating from USNA in 1904, he married the daughter of an admiral and sailed through the ranks, gaining command of a battleship in 1933 and making influential friends on Capitol Hill during his time in the Navy Department. Earlier in his career, he had even briefly served as an aide to Assistant

LEFT | The January 14, 1941, cover of *Look* magazine perfectly, if inadvertently, captured the priorities of President Franklin D. Roosevelt and Americans. FDR's eyes are focused on Europe. Japan is a second thought, if that.

Secretary of the Navy Franklin D. Roosevelt, a post that undoubtedly worked to his advantage in the 1930s.

But more than contacts advanced his career. He was a spit-and-shine, by-the-book Navy Man, dedicated, hard working, loyal, and conscientious. He made rear admiral in 1937 as a result of his accomplishments; on February 1, 1941, as a full admiral, he leapfrogged over higher-ranking officers and became CinCPAC because he was perhaps the best man for the assignment.

Kimmel's luck changed dramatically and irreversibly on December 7, 1941 as a result of misfortune that was not of his making. The Japanese assault against Pearl Harbor did not finish off the American base, but it ended Kimmel's naval career. During the congressional investigation after the war, Kimmel's statements left the crucial question unanswered for many of the committee members.

During a lunch break, Edward Morgan, a lawyer who would write the majority report, asked Kimmel why, after he had received several general warnings, he kept the Fleet in Pearl Harbor? Tired of the same accusations and interrogations, Kimmel answered, "All right, Morgan—I'll give you your answer. I never thought those yellow sons-of-bitches could pull off such an attack, so far from Japan."

Throughout the decade before Pearl Harbor, the United States had consistently misjudged Japan's potential as a dangerous military power. As noted, focus on the economic troubles at home was only part of the answer, but that focus led many American officials to overlook early Japanese aggression in Manchuria and China. It should be remembered that during most of the 1930s, Japan, not China, was the United States' leading market in Asia. Japan purchased far more American steel and oil than did China. United States' policy makers strove diplomatically to encourage Japan to behave peacefully in international affairs, but only later in the decade did America apply trade sanctions.

ABOVE | Admiral Husband Kimmel had led a charmed life until the Japanese assault on Pearl Harbor ended his navy career. Later he tried to explain what went wrong, but never satisfactorily enough for investigators.

Racism was another factor. Americans at the time, including some of the nation's military leaders, often referred to the Japanese as "little yellow men," a phrase that is loaded with meaning. "Yellow" implied alien and potentially threatening. The notion of the "Yellow Peril" had been around for decades. But "little" tended to negate the threat by indicating that Japanese men were small in stature, and therefore less manly, and that Japanese culture was insignificant compared to Euro-American culture.

Perhaps the major reason, however, was the simple fact that during the 1930s, American politics and culture looked east toward Europe and not west toward Asia. This had always been so. Although America had expanded toward the Pacific Ocean, and its concept of manifest destiny had been largely directed toward the Great Plains and West Coast, its cultural cues, ideas, and inspirations flowed primarily from Europe. More than a century after George Washington had warned his countrymen to "beware of foreign entanglements," few had heeded his advice. America was deeply entangled in European economic, political, and cultural affairs, and events in Asia took a backseat to the crisis on "the Continent."

By 1937, when Japan went to war with China, President Roosevelt and the State

Department were fully occupied with the multiplying crises in Europe, from the Italian conquest of Ethiopia, the German reoccupation of the Rhineland, and the German and Soviet involvement in the Spanish Civil War to Adolf Hitler's forced *Anschluss* with Austria, acquisition of the Sudetenland in Czechoslovakia, and finally invasion of Poland, Denmark, the Low Countries, and France.

Japan was a problem, certainly, but a minor one compared to the foreign policy mess that Hitler had created. Without question, almost to the eve of Pearl Harbor, Roosevelt believed he could handle Japan with carrot-and-stick diplomacy. Japan needed American oil, high-grade aviation fuel, scrap

ABOVE | World War II propaganda posters captured the temper of American racism. Japanese are pictured variously as subhuman and inhuman, but never really fully human.

iron, and steel, and Roosevelt assumed that if he embargoed those goods he could force Japan to behave in a less aggressive manner. By the second half of 1941, as he devoted increasing time to the undeclared naval war with Germany on the Atlantic, he believed that negotiations would solve the problems with Japan.

Surely, FDR thought, Japan would not attack the United States. It would be suicidal. There was no way Japan could win such a conflict. In the summer of 1941, Admiral Harold R. Stark, Roosevelt's Chief of Naval Operations (CNO), bluntly made the case to Japanese ambassador Admiral Nomura Kichisaburo, explaining, "While you may have your initial successes . . . the time will come when you, too, will have your losses, but . . . you will not only be unable to make up your losses but will grow weaker as time goes on . . . we will not only make up our losses but will grow stronger as time goes on.

ABOVE | Diplomats Kichisaburo Nomura and Saburo Kurusu are all smiles after an early December 1941 meeting with Secretary of State Cordell Hull. But nothing in the "peace" talks provided any reason for optimism.

Americans increasingly understood the importance of blocking Japan's territorial ambitions. But at what price? The people were divided. A 1941 Gallup poll conducted from October 24 through 29 asked, "Should the United States take steps now to prevent Japan from becoming more powerful even if this means risking a war with Japan?" Nearly two-thirds surveyed said yes. A poll taken from November 27 to December 1 asked, "Do you think the United States will go to war against Japan sometime in the near future?" Just over half said yes, while only 27 percent said no and 21 percent registered no opinion.

It is inevitable that we shall crush you before we are through with you."

Stark's logic did not account for Japanese passion. *Yamato-damashii*—"the brave, daring, and indomitable spirit of the Japanese people"—was Japan's answer to the cold logic of American policy makers. The Japanese had their own manifest destiny, their own beliefs that they, above all people, were favored by the gods. It was an ideal that millions of Japanese were willing to die for. They wondered: Did the same national will exist in America?

Although hardly resounding cries for war, such figures would have been unthinkable a few years earlier. A series of Neutrality Acts passed in the mid-1930s, before Japan's 1937 invasion of China and Germany's 1939 march into Poland, aimed to shelter the United States from potential overseas entanglements. Once again, the debate was primarily framed in European terms. Collectively, the Neutrality Acts forbade American corporations from selling weapons to nations at war, required that warring states purchase nonmilitary goods in cash and transport them in their own ships, and advised citizens

ABOVE | Admiral Harold R. Stark accurately predicted the course of the Pacific War. Japan might score a few early victories, but in the end the United States would win the war.

ABOVE | The ghosts of World War I haunted the Roosevelt administration. The Neutrality Acts of the mid-1930s limited FDR's ability to maneuver in world affairs, especially at a time when Germany threatened France and Britain.

that they travel to war zones at their own risk—the government took no responsibility for their safety. Isolationist congressmen specifically designed the Neutrality Acts to avoid the issues that embroiled United States in the First World War. This time around, they thought, there would be no *Lusitania*s, and no American bankers seeking repayment of loans extended to arms-hungry Europeans.

The outbreak of war in Europe in September 1939 produced a declaration of American neutrality and an effort by President Roosevelt to set the terms of that neutrality. Roosevelt asked Congress to lift the arms embargo, a move that would have enabled a flow of weapons into France and Great Britain. "Is not this laying the foundation for intervention?" asked isolationist Senator Willam Borah of Idaho. "Why trifle with foreign war?" he continued. "Why bring the American boys to the precipice where any incident of war may kick them over?"

A heated debate in Congress aroused similar passions around the United States. One of those spurred to action was Charles Lindbergh, the celebrated aviator who, despite yearning for privacy, was one of the most famous men in the world. Lindbergh had visited Nazi Germany and come away impressed with its strength, particularly its powerful *Luftwaffe*. He did not side with the

Germans in the conflict, but he also did not see why the United States should stumble its way into the fight. "We must band together to prevent the loss of more American lives in these internal struggles of Europe," he advised a national radio audience on September 15. "We must keep foreign propaganda from pushing our country blindly into another war."

Unfortunately, Lindbergh inserted some questionable racial sentiments into his appeal for isolation, inadvertently but clearly expressing his attitude toward Japan and Asia. "These wars in Europe are not wars in which our civilization is defending itself against some Asiatic intruder," he declared. "This is not a question of banding together to defend the white race against foreign invasion."

ABOVE | Although Charles Lindbergh's transatlantic flight seemed to shrink the world, before World War II he argued against American involvement in the European conflict.

New York Post

WEATHER
Partly cloudy and continued cool tonight and tomorrow. Fresh northwest winds diminishing tomorrow. Lowest temperature tonight 58 degrees.

BLUE FINAL
RACES — BOX SCORES
PAGES 12 AND 13

Founded 1801, Volume 139, No. 235.
Copyright 1940, New York Post, Inc.

NEW YORK TUESDAY AUGUST 20 1940

THREE CENTS

CHURCHILL OFFERS BASES TO U. S., ASKS DESTROYERS

Declares Britain Outbuilds Germany in Planes

BRITISH SOURCES SAY:

HUNDREDS OF PLANES BOMB BRITAIN

Flynn Calls Willkie Unstable for Denying Proved Tammany Tie

CERTIFICATE OF ELECTION TO COUNTY COMMITTEE
BOARD OF ELECTIONS IN THE CITY OF NEW YORK

Profits Drive Holds Up 5,725 Planes

Arnold Tells Senators British Contracts Are Taken Before America's

WASHINGTON, Aug. 20 (UP).

Hitler in France; Invasion Is Near; More Chutes Land

Although the following dispatch does not make any definite assertion that the Germans have succeeded in landing parachutists in Britain, it nevertheless strongly implies that such is the case.

Miss Kirkpatrick, who yesterday revealed that Britain was abandoning Somaliland, several hours before the official announcement of that fact, possesses unusual

Dog-Fights Rage 2 Hours Over England

Coast Rocks With Numerous Blasts—Balloon Raiders Routed

By WILLIAM H. STONEMAN
Special Cable to The Post

LONDON, Aug. 20 (UP).—Prime Minister Churchill today told Commons that Britain is stronger than ever despite Germany's furious air attacks, and that Britain's new plane production "already has largely exceeded Germany's."

"British airmen," he said, "are turning the tide of war."

Churchill also declared:

1. Britain was prepared to offer to the U. S. 99-year leases on air and naval bases in Newfoundland and the West Indies.

(In the House of Lords tonight, Foreign Secretary Halifax said an agreement in principle already had been reached with the U. S. on the bases.)

2. He hoped the U. S. would release its over-age destroyers to bolster Britain's defenses.

3. The blockade of all Europe would be maintained despite appeals to permit shipments of American food supplies to France, Belgium and Holland.

4. British casualties to date in the war totaled 92,000,

Both Lindbergh and Borah presented the war as a European phenomenon. So did the deliberations in Congress. Japan barely even registered as a second priority. Hitler was the greater threat, and was therefore the focus of the national conversation.

Congress voted to lift the arms embargo in 1939. This not only gave hope to the European democracies, but also amplified the volume of the emerging Great Debate over the role of the United States in the European war. Roosevelt and his backers argued that the Axis nations—which did not yet include Japan—had global ambitions that needed to be thwarted lest Americans find themselves in a hostile world dominated by totalitarianism. Noninterventionists charged the president and his allies with leading a reckless crusade that would cause an unfathomable number of American deaths. Better to focus on defending ourselves, they said, and let the rest of the world sort out its own troubles.

The fall of Norway, Denmark, Belgium, the Netherlands, and France in the spring and summer of 1940 drove Roosevelt to pursue additional measures against the Nazis. That autumn, he negotiated the destroyers-for-bases deal with Great Britain, exchanging a fleet of decrepit warships for a string of safe harbors stretching from Newfoundland to the Caribbean. This deal struck a blow for

ABOVE | The autumn 1940 destroyers-for-bases deal was President Roosevelt's attempt to provide needed military aid to Great Britain. At that time Germany was bombing British cities.

hemispheric defense while intertwining the fates of Britain and the United States. At around the same time, Congress passed a bill creating a peacetime draft, again in the name of defending the Americas. Japan played only a minor role in these debates, which remained fixated on Hitler and Germany.

Determined to halt what seemed like an inevitable march into the fight, a Yale law student named Robert Douglas "Bob" Stuart, Jr. organized the Committee to Defend America First. An heir to the Quaker Oats fortune, Stuart recruited some friends, including fellow law student Gerald R. Ford and Sears-Roebuck chairman Robert S. Wood, who believed in creating a strong national defense while eschewing intervention in Europe. Involvement in Asia wasn't even on the table.

America First attracted adherents from across the ideological spectrum. Although a scattering of communists and Nazi sympathizers joined its ranks, most of its eight hundred thousand members were solidly within the political mainstream. Teddy Roosevelt's daughter Alice Roosevelt Longworth joined, as did Walt Disney, poet e e cummings, and World War I flying ace Eddie Rickenbacker.

In April 1941, Lindbergh bolstered the cause with a string of successful speeches. He drew rapturous applause from an audience of ten thousand in the Chicago Arena. A similar crowd greeted him in Manhattan less than a week later. Fifteen thousand people turned out in St. Louis. Twenty-five thousand showed up at Madison Square Garden, while an equal number heard the aviator's speech projected from loudspeakers erected outside the building.

The enthusiastic crowds at America First events represented only one side of the argument. Applause mixed with boos and hisses whenever Lindbergh's face appeared in a newsreel. Opponents such as the Committee to Defend America by Aiding the Allies accused America Firsters of being closet Nazis. Rumors spread that Lindbergh was

ABOVE | Established in September 1940 at Yale University, the Committee to Defend America First was dedicated to keeping the United States from drifting into the European war.

ABOVE | Students at the University of California, Berkeley, engaged in a one-day peace strike against US involvement in the European war. They supported the efforts of the America First Committee.

actually a Nazi spy, or the head of a spy ring, or in some other way mixed up in nefarious affairs. Roosevelt generally stayed above the fray but occasionally flung a barb at the isolationists or tweaked Lindbergh as an appeaser, a stinging accusation at the time.

Noninterventionist groups such as America First had powerful allies in Congress, none more vocal than Senators Burton K. Wheeler of Montana and Gerald Nye of North Dakota. Although Wheeler was a Democrat and Nye a Republican, both viewed Roosevelt as hell-bent on driving the country into the European fight. The president is "blitzkrieging the American people into this war," Nye warned in May 1941. Wheeler, a longtime foe of big business, suggested that "economic royalists" were maneuvering FDR into firing the first shot.

By mid-1941, as Roosevelt was tightening the economic screws on Japan through a series of trade embargoes, the Great Debate increasingly revolved around whether the mass media was biased in favor of aiding Great Britain. It is hard to imagine an alternative. American news outlets could hardly have tilted pro-Axis, and coverage of Great Britain during the blitz was bound to elicit sympathy. Radioman Edward R. Murrow's broadcasts from bombed-out London encouraged listeners to see international

events through the eyes of the plucky Brits who slept in subway stations before emerging the next morning to find out whether their homes were still standing.

Who are "the major war agitators in this country?" Lindbergh asked at a September 1941 America First rally in Des Moines. The

ABOVE | While Americans debated involvement in the war, the British were all in. Newsman and radio commentator Edward R. Murrow (above) reported the war from London, poignantly describing the British plight, including scenes from the Blitz (below). In his own way, Murrow brought the horrors of war home to American listeners.

British, the Roosevelt administration, and the Jews, he claimed. Speaking of Jews, the flyer observed that "their greatest danger to this country lies in their large ownership and influence in our motion pictures, our press, our radio, and our government."

Lindbergh's passionate defense of non-interventionism found traction, especially in the Midwest, where other voices joined his. Senator Nye had loosed a similar attack not long before. "Who has brought us to the verge of war?" Nye asked a national radio audience. In his mind, one of the main culprits was Hollywood. "The truth is that in twenty thousand theaters in the United States tonight they are holding war mass meetings," he thundered. He claimed Hollywood was run by a certain kind of person. They came from "Russia, Hungary, Germany, and the Balkan countries." Not only did they come from Eastern Europe, they were *Jews* from Eastern Europe.

Overseas events had turned the United States into an angry brew of charges and countercharges, political infighting and paranoia, skepticism and suspicion. Hollywood executives had no desire to get drawn into the fray. Like most Americans, the movie colony almost unanimously opposed the Axis. A few stars, including James Cagney, Melvyn Douglas, and Douglas Fairbanks, Jr., had publicly criticized the Nazis. But the studios were far more interested in making money than in making enemies. If promoting rearmament sold tickets, then they would make movies about rearmament. If flag-waving paeans to democracy did the same, then overt patriotism would be the order of the day.

Germany dominated Hollywood's attention. Nazi villains were starting to creep into films, including such notables as *Confessions of a Nazi Spy* (1939), *The Mortal Storm* (1940), and *Man Hunt* (1941), along with Charlie Chaplin's classic *The Great Dictator* (1940). The Japanese remained as absent from the screen as they were in many people's minds.

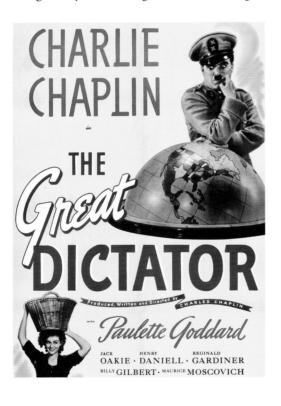

Columbia Pictures inadvertently captured the differences between Americans' views of Germans and Japanese in July 1941 when it released the Three Stooges short *I'll Never Heil Again*. The comedy features Moe Howard playing the leader of Moronica; he's a tyrant who happens to look just like Adolf Hitler. "Moronica for Morons" reads a banner displaying Moronica's national symbol: two snakes contorted into a swastika.

Following the usual Stooge-related hijinks and hilarity, dictator Moe gathers his allies for the revelation of his grand strategy. "Your blitz is on the fritz," he declares, "I am the winner and the world belongs to me!" The unnamed representative from Japan—of course, no one ever *says* he's from Japan, although the resemblance with Emperor Hirohito is obvious—leaps up in protest. "Oh no," he shouts with a heavy accent, "dat's bery, bery unjust, please. Sank you!" It's his only line in the film, and one that establishes him as a

ABOVE | In *I'll Never Heil Again* (1941), the Three Stooges also made fun of Adolf Hitler, suggesting that his followers in Germany were "morons." Although slow to take a position, Hollywood was speaking out more forcefully against Hitler.

41

second banana in the alliance. His excessive politeness is ridiculous. They are the words of a man incapable of doing more than squeaking whenever things don't go his way.

Beyond this cameo, almost no Japanese characters appeared in movies made in the late 1930s and very early 1940s. It was as if the Japanese weren't even worth worrying about when the Germans were busy redrawing the map of Europe. Their onscreen invisibility both confirmed and encouraged Americans' longstanding stereotypes of the Japanese as a childlike, primitive people beneath the notice of a civilized nation.

Hollywood churned out productions parroting Roosevelt's foreign policy. Preparedness was the watchword of the day. *The Fighting 69th* (1940) transformed the brutal and divisive World War I into a lesson about national unity. "There's no room in this rainbow for sectional feuds," Colonel William "Wild Bill" Donovan tells his division, made up of soldiers from every part of the country, "because we're all one nation now, one team. An all-American team pulling together, and known as the United States Army."

ABOVE | During World War II, Hollywood portrayed an America that was unified along ethnic, racial, class, and gender lines. *The Fighting 69th* (1940) blazed the trail for other war films. Its theme was all-American unity.

Warner Bros. released *Sergeant York* in July 1941, the same month *I'll Never Heil Again* hit theaters. A biopic of World War I hero Alvin York, who became famous when he helped capture 132 German soldiers during the 1917 Meuse-Argonne offensive, the film became the year's highest-grossing movie. Secretary of State Cordell Hull telegrammed his best wishes on opening night.

The War Department loaned its star, Gary Cooper, a Medal of Honor to wear during filming.

Sergeant York made no effort to conceal its true purpose of convincing a peaceful nation that it sometimes must fight to defend its freedoms. York is a patriotic man whose religion teaches him that killing is wrong. When the army drafts him, he struggles to reconcile

ABOVE | In *Sergeant York* (1941), Gary Cooper played the World War I hero Alvin York. A reluctant hero, York overcame religious concerns and embraced America's war in Europe.

the demands of his God with the needs of his country. He retreats to a mountaintop so he can sort through his moral crisis. With the words of his major ("your country") and his pastor ("your God") echoing in his mind, he sees that the wind has blown open his Bible to Matthew 22:21: "Render therefore unto Caesar the things which are Caesar's; and unto God the things that are God's." This divine intervention solves his dilemma. "My Country 'Tis of Thee" swells, York embraces military life, and audiences gain assurance that morality and war sometimes went hand in hand.

Hollywood was "seemingly reenacting the war propaganda role played by the movies prior to the last war," anti-interventionist congressman Lewis Thill of Wisconsin

complained. Enough of his colleagues agreed that in September 1941 a subcommittee of the Senate Interstate Commerce Committee opened hearings on the topic of propaganda in the movie industry. Senators Wheeler and Nye, the body's two most vocal anti-interventionists, played key roles in arranging the inquiry.

Noninterventionists planned on using the hearings as a platform for their views while tarring their ideological opponents as bloodthirsty warmongers. Instead, the probe became an embarrassment. Senator Nye sounded more anti-Semitic every time he explained that he was not an anti-Semite. His peers admitted that they had not seen any of the movies they denounced as propaganda. Hollywood's defense counsel, Wendell Willkie, the Republican Party's presidential nominee in 1940, successfully wrapped the industry in the garb of American liberty and freedom of speech.

Warner Bros. head Harry Warner dominated the hearings with his unapologetic testimony. "I am opposed to Nazism," he declared. "I abhor and detest every principle and practice of the Nazi movement." His studio would oppose the Axis, he informed his questioners, who by that point were trying hard to melt into their chairs.

The hearings disintegrated without

ABOVE | Alvin York (Gary Cooper) discusses the conflict between his pacifist religion and the need for national self-defense in 1941's blockbuster *Sergeant York*.

finding any coordinated campaign on Hollywood's part to pull the United States into the war. It did, however, expose the wide gaps in American public opinion. People were nervous, twitchy, and touchy. War seemed like both an abomination and an inevitability.

The senators never asked about the film industry's views on Japan. But in the White House, one mile up Pennsylvania Avenue from the hearings in the Capitol, Japan was very much on the minds of the Roosevelt administration and top military officials. Relations with Japan were growing increasingly hostile and were clearly approaching a crisis point. FDR and his advisors expected a provocative move from Japan at any moment. But the rest of the country was looking in the opposite direction, gazing at Hitler's Germany, their backs toward the Empire of the Rising Sun.

ABOVE | Warner Bros. cast anti-Nazi German expatriate Martin Kosleck as German propaganda minister Joseph Goebbels in the studio's 1939 anti-Nazi film *Confessions of a Nazi Spy.*

CHAPTER 3
A GAMBLER'S PLAN

It was a time of hard choices. By the beginning of 1941 Japan's leaders faced the fact that they were racing toward a crossroads, and the direction they took would determine their country's future. For almost a decade the expansionists in the military had dominated the Imperial Council, approving the moves into Manchuria and China in the hopes of acquiring the raw materials their country lacked. And the war in Europe played into Japan's hands, opening new avenues of expansion. When Adolf Hitler's armies overran the Netherlands and France, Japan began to covet the French and Dutch—even the British—empires in Asia and the Pacific.

Indochina with its rice, Malaya with its rubber and tin, and the Dutch East Indies with its seemingly boundless holdings of oil, beckoned. In addition, Britain's war against Germany made it difficult for Churchill's islands to protect their interests in Malaya, Singapore, Hong Kong, Burma, and India.

Expansion to build an empire appeared to be the answer to Japan's troubles. Japan had matured as a Pacific power, modeling its development in part on the pattern of Great Britain, another island nation dependent on overseas holdings to power its economy. No political philosopher was more important in Japan than Alfred Thayer Mahan, the

LEFT | Recruiting posters seeking aviators for the Imperial Japanese Navy linked flying with patriotism. Everything, it suggests, was done for the greater glory of the nation.

47

American geopolitical strategist who argued that sea power and overseas empires were the surest route to national prosperity and security. Indeed, for officers in the Imperial Japanese Navy, Mahan's classic text, *The Influence of Sea Power upon History, 1660–1783*, was required reading. Without expansion, policy makers contended, Japan would be eternally dependent on the United States, a vassal nation subject to American whims and priorities.

Two treaties signaled Japan's intentions. First, on November 27, 1940, Japan signed the Tripartite Pact with Germany and Italy, a political, economic, and military treaty that targeted the United States. Tokyo hoped the treaty would signal Japanese strength and

deter American ambitions in Asia. As Prime Minister Prince Fumimaro Konoe insisted, "a humble attitude will only prompt the United States to become domineering," so "a demonstration of strength is necessary." Second, on April 13, 1941, Japan inked the Japanese-Soviet Non-Aggression Pact, pledging neutrality between the two nations. The treaty safeguarded Japan's northern border, permitting Tokyo to initiate expansion toward the south.

The treaties provided Japanese with fascist allies and alleviated the problems of a two-front war, but they also increased the likelihood of hostilities with the United States. Japanese policy makers, particularly those in the army and navy, tended to be narrow-minded and provincial, quick to look for military solutions to political, economic, and diplomatic problems. At virtually every step of the way they miscalculated America's response. For example, Japan viewed the Tripartite Pact as a deterrent; US policy makers considered it the act of a bullying, belligerent, imperialistic nation. To American eyes, Japan was an Asian version of Nazi Germany, blindly grabbing all the territory it could get its hands on. With the lessons of Munich and appeasement fresh in American minds, the United States felt it had to stand up to a bully. Appeasement was

ABOVE | Historian and naval officer Admiral Alfred Thayer Mahan wrote about the importance of sea power in world affairs. His classic study *The Influence of Sea Power upon History, 1660–1783* was required reading for Japanese naval officers.

ABOVE | German foreign minister Joachim von Ribbentrop reads a statement after the signing of the Tripartite Pact with Italy and Japan. Representatives, including Adolf Hitler, of the three nations look on.

a futile approach, even though President Roosevelt's policy toward Japan attempted to mix strength with flexibility.

Relations between the United States and Japan continued to deteriorate throughout 1941. Hoping to end its costly and bloody war with China, Japan pressured France and, for a time, Britain to close supply routes from Indochina and Burma into China. FDR viewed these actions as a prelude to Japan's attempt to extend its control in Southeast Asia, and in July, America slapped an embargo on selling aviation fuel, high-grade iron, and scrap steel to Japan. More embargoes followed, but Japan continued to encroach on Southeast Asia.

The United States and Japan were playing a high-stakes game of tit for tat. An action by one nation drew an immediate response by the other. Soon the FDR administration had embargoed all the goods Japan needed, frozen Japan's assets in the United States, and convinced Britain and the Netherlands to go along with the penalties. And since Japan imported 88 percent of its oil and much of its other needed resources, Tokyo turned ever more expansionist. It soon became clear to policy makers in both Japan and the United States that the game could not drag on indefinitely.

Japanese leaders saw only three alternatives. The first dictated capitulation. They could abandon their plans for Southeast Asia, withdraw from China, and table their imperial dreams. The second entailed compromise. They could negotiate with the United States from a position of weakness and work out a resumption of trade at the cost of significant concessions. The third, and the riskiest, required war. They could attack British and Dutch possessions in Southeast Asia, as well as American bases in East Asia and the Pacific. It was a gamble, to be sure, but one many Japanese military planners readily accepted.

Japan had ambitions—goals that could be shaped into policy and strategy. At the end of 1940 those ambitions had no operational blueprint, no plan that outlined how Japan could triumph against the Western powers. But an operational blueprint began taking shape in January 1941 when Admiral Isoroku Yamamoto put his incredible intelligence and imagination to the problem. It was then that he started to consider the unimaginable—a war against the immensely larger, significantly more populous, and industrially stronger United States. No person in the Japanese Imperial Navy was better suited for the assignment, and probably none wanted it less.

Yamamoto was born Isoroku Takano in 1884 on the island of Honshu. His father,

Sadayoshi Tanaka, was a hard-pressed schoolmaster with a large family. "My age is fifty-six," he told his wife, "let's call him that." Isoroku is written with the characters for five, ten, and six. Isoroku was almost thirty when his parents died, and already on his way to a successful navy career. In line with the common practice of influential families with no male heir adopting young men to continue their name, Isoroku was taken in by the Yamamoto clan.

He more than made up for the honor. He had been a stellar student at the Etajima Naval Academy, where he lived a spartan regime of abstention from tobacco, alcohol,

and sweets. He graduated near the top of his class and immediately went to sea. In the Russo-Japanese War he served on a cruiser at the Battle of Tsushima Strait, the Japanese navy's defining engagement. When a shell hit his ship, he was knocked unconscious, suffering a leg injury and two severed fingers on his left hand. Had he lost another finger he would have been discharged from the navy as physically unfit, but he stayed in the service and received important military and political assignments.

Twice he was sent to the United States. In 1919 he traveled to Boston, where he studied English at Harvard and learned the

ABOVE | The Battle of Tsushima Strait established Japan as a Pacific power. In an exhibition of seamanship and strategy, Japanese naval leaders outmaneuvered and soundly defeated the Russian fleet.

game of poker from American friends. He loved the challenge of the game, excelling in bluffs and betting. Twice in the 1920s he served as a naval attaché in Washington, DC. Working in the capital and traveling about America, Yamamoto came to respect the nation and understand its industrial might. More parochial officers in Japan disparaged America's racial diversity and cultural laxity, but Yamamoto had no illusions concerning America's strength or the character of its citizens. If war came between Japan and America, he felt, his country would face a nearly unwinnable fight. In January 1941 he cautioned an ultranationalist that if war broke out "it would not be enough that we take

Guam and the Philippines, nor even Hawaii and San Francisco. To make victory certain, we would have to march into Washington and dictate the terms of peace in the White House." He doubted if any of the firebrands in the military grasped the implications of such a war.

Though only five feet three inches tall, and having a placid expression and sensitive eyes, Yamamoto spoke forcefully and to the point in councils of state. If in the long run he proved on the right side of history, he was on the losing side of critical debates of his day. He opposed alliances with Germany and Italy. He distrusted the ability of such politicians as Prince Konoe to guide Japan. And, most of all, he opposed war with the United States. But as the Commander in Chief of Japan's Combined Fleet, his duty required him to follow the orders of the emperor's council. The momentum of Japan's leadership was striding toward expansion and war. Yamamoto understood that the drive toward the Dutch East Indies, Indochina, and Malaya would lead to conflict with Holland and Britain, as well as the United States. His job was to devise a plan that gave Japan the greatest chance of success.

Yamamoto brought to the assignment several general beliefs, some vintage and others new. Like military leaders since the

ABOVE | Admiral Isoroku Yamamoto lost two fingers in the Battle of Tsushima Strait, and by 1941 had risen to Commander in Chief of the Combined Fleet. To him fell the assignment of developing an operational strategy to defeat the United States, a task, he realized, that was virtually impossible.

"I am looking forward to dictating peace to the United States in the White House at Washington"
— ADMIRAL YAMAMOTO

What do YOU say, AMERICA?

ABOVE | Although the Japanese attack on Pearl Harbor was the work of many planners, Admiral Yamamoto came up with the original idea. His audacity runs through the plan.

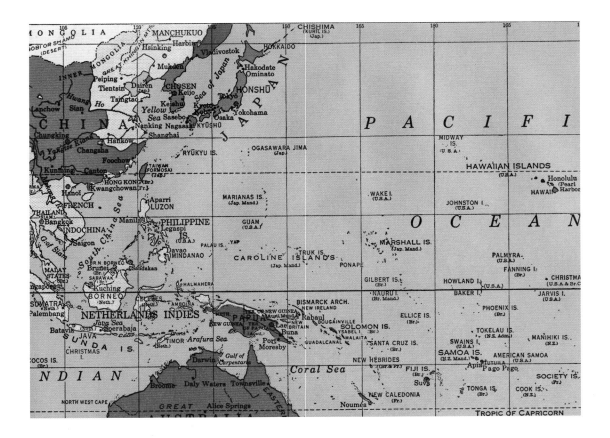

nineteenth century, he was committed to the notion of the "decisive battle," the idea that a war could be won or lost in one climactic engagement. Yet similar to several of his contemporary naval theorists, he endorsed the importance of aircraft carriers and the idea of air power as central to sea warfare. The age of the primacy of battleships, of the "Togo Turn" and "Crossing the T" at the Battle of Tsushima Strait, was rapidly ending. If Japan had a chance of achieving a decisive victory it had to plan and act boldly, surprising and crippling its enemy.

When it was fully formed, his plan en-tailed coordinated, combined naval and army assaults against Western positions in Southeast Asia and the Western Pacific. It included initial attacks against Western bases in Hawaii, the Philippines, Wake Island, Guam, Malaya, Singapore, Thailand, and Hong Kong, followed by later assaults against Burma, the Dutch East Indies, New Guinea, the Solomon Islands, and the cities of Kuala Lumpur and Rabaul. The territorial acquisitions promised to give Japan bases and outposts from which it could establish a defensive perimeter to control the Pacific from Hawaii and Midway north to the Aleutian Islands; west to the Kurile

ABOVE | Japan's military struck at locations across the Pacific in December 1941.

Islands; south past the Ryukyu Islands, the coast of China, Indochina, and Philippines to the Dutch East Indies; and east along New Guinea and the Solomon Islands, to the Gilbert Islands. Japan planned to fortify everything inside the ring and threaten nations just outside, including Australia and India. In its final form, the plan was as outrageously bold as it was ingenious.

The destruction—or at least incapacitation—of the US Pacific Fleet at Pearl Harbor was the centerpiece of the strategy. Yamamoto asserted, "The most important thing we have to do first of all in a war with the

US, I firmly believe, is to fiercely attack and destroy the US main fleet at the outset of the war, so that the morale of the US Navy and her people goes down to such an extent that it cannot be recovered." In addition, he maintained that America's fleet had to be sidelined to give Japan six months to "run wild" in the Western Pacific.

The key elements of this part of the plan were surprise and air power. A veteran of the Russo-Japanese War, and a great admirer of Admiral Heihachiro Togo, Yamamoto's thinking was influenced by Japan's surprise attack and resounding victory against the

Russian Pacific Squadron at the Battle of Port Arthur in 1904. The assault shocked Russian leaders who considered the Japanese little more than hollow imitators of Western military fashions, incapable of mastering complex weaponry or military strategies.

Port Arthur offered a lesson to Western powers dealing with the East. Rudyard Kipling said as much in "The Naulahka," a poem that suggested,

> *And the end of the fight is a tombstone*
> *   white with the name of the late deceased,*
> *And the epitaph drear: "A fool lies here*
> *   who tried to hustle the East."*

But the lesson had been poorly learned. Shortly after the successful surprise attack

ABOVE | This chart of Pearl Harbor, recovered from a Japanese midget submarine captured during the attack, demonstrates the minute level of planning that went into the assault.

on Pearl Harbor, Yamamoto wrote a friend's son, a student, explaining, "That we could defeat the enemy at the outbreak of the war was because they were unguarded and also they made light of us. 'Danger comes soonest when it is despised,' and 'don't despise a small enemy' are really important matters."

The day and the time—more than the date—of the attack were critical. It had to be on a Sunday morning, Yamamoto maintained. He was familiar with American customs, especially those of sailors. He knew that on Sunday mornings sailors would either be singing at a church service or sleeping off

a Saturday night drunk. Sundays were slow days at Pearl—senior officers played golf or tennis, meals after service ran long, sailors relaxed over coffee as they recounted their previous night's adventures. It was in most respects a day off.

No one would expect death to rain from the sky. But Yamamoto knew that was the only way to reach the American fleet at Pearl Harbor. He could send a Japanese carrier strike force undetected across the virtually deserted north Pacific, and it could launch torpedo planes, high-level and dive-bombers, and fighters from 200 to 220 miles away

ABOVE | Aboard the Japanese carrier *Kaga*, Lieutenant Ichiro Kitajima briefs his flight crew about the Pearl Harbor assault. In 1942, the *Kaga* was scuttled after being crippled during the Battle of Midway.

from the target. Hundreds of planes—perhaps four to five hundred—could achieve a surprise victory over a sleepy, overconfident, and unprepared American force. It would be Yamamoto's Port Arthur. The attack would shift the balance of power in the Pacific in Japan's favor, protecting its drive into resource-rich Southeast Asia and solving its basic military needs.

The plan was not fully conceived when it was hatched. Yamamoto wrote out the basic outline and then solicited opinions and ideas from other naval planners. Rear Admiral Takijiro Onishi, a brilliant exponent of carrier warfare and master at working out the tactical details of plans, refined Yamamoto's ideas. Commander Kosei Maeda applied himself to the problem of aerial torpedo warfare. "A torpedo attack against US warships at Pearl Harbor, from a technical standpoint alone, would be virtually impossible" he said. "The water of the base is too shallow." And attacks by dive-bombers entailed significant, perhaps fatal, risks.

At the behest of Onishi, Commander Minoru Genda took a look at the plans. Genda, virtually everyone agreed, was a genius on the subject of naval air power. Born in 1904 near Hiroshima, the dark-eyed, intense officer bristled against the naval battleship establishment and did not

suffer fools gladly. After graduating from the Imperial Japanese Naval Academy at Etajima, he trained as a fighter pilot and led the famous "Genda's Flying Circus," a team of high-risk aerobatic flyers who thrilled the public at air shows and promoted naval aviation. He was the Japanese Billy Mitchell, America's leading advocate of air power. Even more than Yamamoto, he insisted that carrier groups would dominate the next war. The age of battleships was over, he argued, and Japan's leaders should place their faith—and spend their money—on aircraft carriers. But he was still too young to have much influence, though he did become widely recognized as a spokesman for naval air power. His opinion was highly valued by Yamamoto's team.

Onishi outlined Yamamoto's design, finally handing Genda the Commander in Chief's proposal. Genda read it carefully, admiringly. Its audacity and brilliance appealed to his daredevil nature. Onishi waited for Genda to finish, knowing that the young officer would give an unvarnished opinion.

"The plan is difficult but not impossible," Genda said. It might—just might—be the answer to all of Japan's economic, military, and strategic troubles. It offered a way to acquire essential resources and end the war

ABOVE | Propaganda poster of Japanese airman dating from 1944 or 1945. By then the Japanese air forces were in shambles.

in China. It was a plan for domination of the Pacific and leadership of Asia.

Genda threw his energies into refining the plan. He, too, believed in the necessity of an early-morning surprise attack, though he believed the mission should prioritize the destruction of US carriers and land-based planes on Oahu. And since he wanted to inflict maximum damage, he advocated the use of a large carrier force. Like Maeda, however, he doubted if torpedo planes could effectively attack ships in such shallow waters.

After offering his appraisal of the plan, Genda started to work on the torpedo problem. Instead of landing, stabilizing, and tracking toward their targets, traditional torpedoes plunged into the water and buried in the mud of the harbor floor. At Lahaina Roads, a deeper port where the American fleet occasionally harbored, there was sufficient depth for conventional torpedoes, but Genda knew he had to prepare to attack the more difficult target.

Searching for an answer, he worked with a longtime friend, Commander Mitsuo Fuchida. A specialist in horizontal bombing, Fuchida was two years older than Genda and as committed to aerial naval warfare. He was a brave, daring pilot, who would soon be selected to lead the air assaults on Pearl Harbor. Together, pilots and research teams led by Fuchida and Genda experimented

ABOVE | World War II *kamikaze* pilots committed to sacrificing their lives in furtherance of a doomed cause. By the time of their missions the Japanese air force and navy were virtually destroyed.

with shallow-depth torpedo attacks. While Fuchida trained torpedo pilots to deliver their "fish" at dangerously low altitudes, Genda's group worked on the puzzle of devising a torpedo that stabilized at a depth of about thirty-six feet. Fuchida's labors were difficult and perilous, but successful; Genda's work was frustrating and for a time unrewarding.

Japan's standard 91 Model 2 torpedoes penetrated too deeply into the water, generally to a depth of sixty-five feet. Fuchida's pilots developed techniques to improve the performance, but could not reach the thirty-three to thirty-six feet requirement. Finally technicians working with Genda developed a "fish" with added wooden fins. In theory, the

fins would add buoyancy and stability, and, most importantly, track straight through shallower water. In October 1941 the improved torpedoes were tested. Flying above the test site, Fuchida watched as three of the "fish" were launched. One hit bottom. The other two stabilized and skimmed toward their targets. Two out of three successes, Fuchida calculated, meant twenty-seven hits out of forty launches. The depth problem had been solved.

By the fall, Yamamoto's planning had boiled down to solving various technical issues—such matters as harbor depth, refueling logistics, potential antitorpedo nets, and distance of attack flights—and training for the mission. Although efforts were made to

ABOVE | Japanese bombers in the imaginations of the Japanese people on the home front. Civilians believed the government's propaganda, the idea that Japan controlled the seas and skies.

keep the specifics of the plan to attack Pearl Harbor secret, the general idea had oozed out of official circles and was a subject of discussion among Western diplomats in Tokyo. In late January 1941, US ambassador Joseph Grew, a veteran Japan watcher, wrote Washington, "My Peruvian Colleague told a member of my staff that he had heard from many sources including a Japanese source that the Japanese military forces planned, in event of trouble with the United States, to attempt a surprise mass attack on Pearl Harbor using all of their military facilities." The rumor hardly created a ripple of interest in the State Department or War Department.

Leaders there judged that such an attack would be suicidal.

If the plan was not exactly a recipe for suicide, it did skim close to being an invitation for disaster. There were so many places that it could crash and burn. The strike fleet could run into problems in the north Pacific; it could be spotted and reported; it could be surprised by an enemy force. And if it did cross several thousand miles of the ocean undetected, there was no guarantee that it would discover American battleships and aircraft carriers in or near Pearl Harbor. Yamamoto's final plan depended on destroying or at least critically damaging the American

ABOVE | Joseph Grew, American ambassador to Japan, had caught wind of the plan long before the attack on Pearl Harbor. But his warning went unheeded in Washington, DC.

Pacific Fleet. But that was easier said than done in a shallow harbor, where battered ships could be repaired and refloated.

Perhaps, as some officers in the Japanese and American military believed, such a plan was foolhardy, the dream of adventurous leaders enamored with carriers and air power and not afraid to gamble everything on a weak hand. What Fuchida said about Genda also applied to Yamamoto and several of his supporters: "Genda was sometimes . . . too risky in his judgment when he should have been more careful. . . . He was a man of brilliant ideas. Sometimes, however, his ideas were too flashy." *Risky, flashy*—they are not words suited to sober war plans, especially ones aimed at a country with the population, resources, and strength of the United States.

And there were more judicious minds in Japan. In October 1940 the Japanese Institute of Total War Studies brought together thirty of the nation's "brightest and best" thinkers, recruited from the army, navy, government agencies, leading businesses, and the press. They were given access to top-secret information and told to study the prospects of a continuing war with China and a potential war with the United States. They concluded that Japan lacked the manpower and economic resources to continue to battle China, and that after five or ten years the

drain would become devastating. The group also concluded that Japan could never win a war against the United States. In just a matter of a few years such a conflict would undermine the Japanese economy and society.

The Institute's massive report was delivered to Japan's cabinet in the summer of 1941. On August 27, 1941, members of the committee made presentations to the cabinet, including Prime Minister Fumimaro Konoe and War Minister Hideki Tojo.

The Institute's report was eerily accurate, prescient in its analysis. It was also ignored. Yamamoto's plan carried the day.

ABOVE | Prime Minister Fumimaro Konoe vacillated between talk of war and attempts to preserve the peace. As a son of the Japanese aristocracy, he was more a man of ideas than actions.

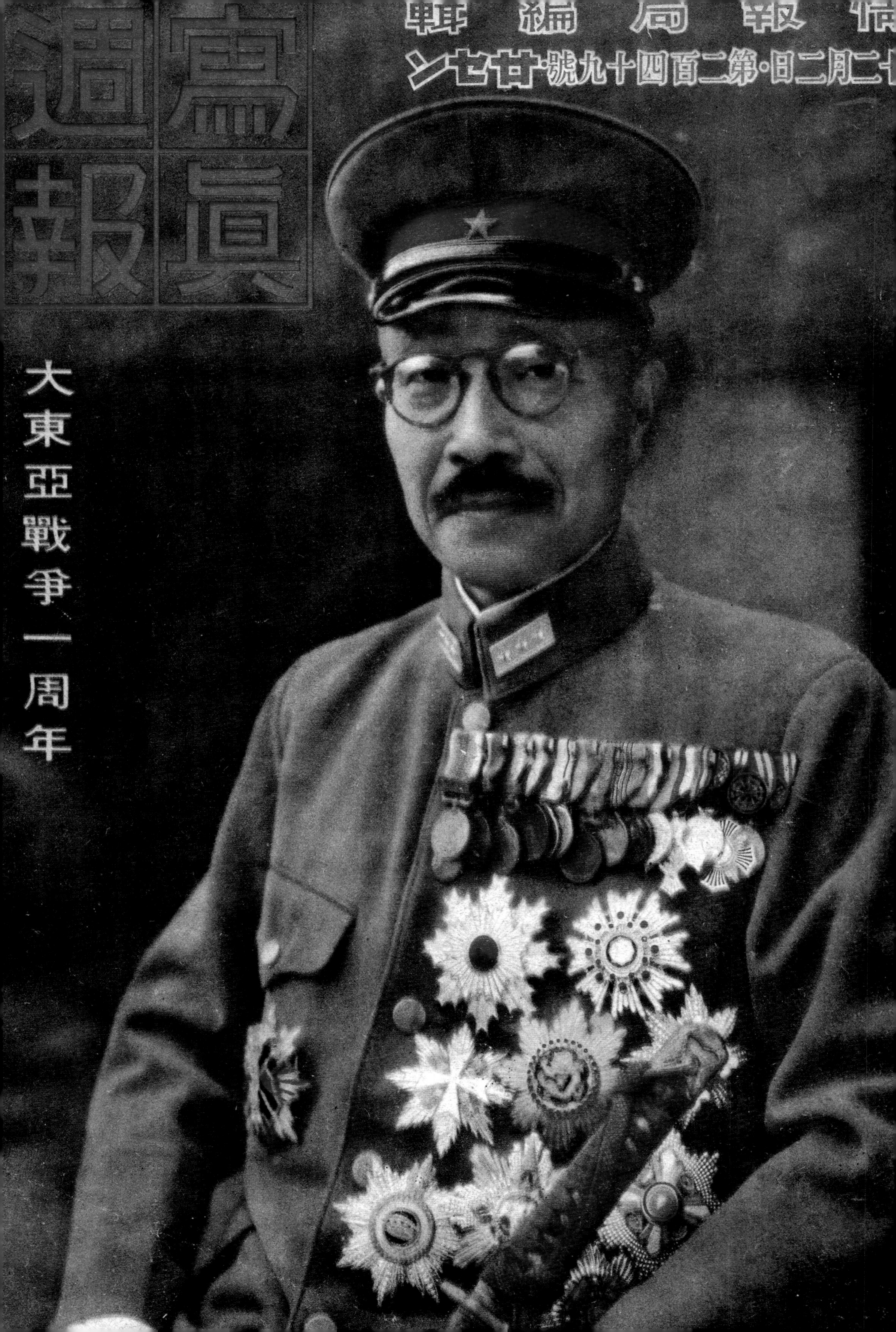
寫眞週報
情報局編輯
十二月二日・第二百四十九號・廿セン
大東亞戰爭一周年

CHAPTER 4
LAST CHANCES

On November 5, 1941 the luminaries of the Japanese government assembled in the First Eastern Hall of the Meiji Palace for an imperial conference. As always, the room looked magnificent. Glass chandeliers hung from the ceiling and purple silks embroidered with flower designs adorned the walls. Emperor Hirohito sat silently, as tradition dictated. Hideki Tojo, prime minister for all of seventeen days, held the floor while Foreign Minister Shigenori Togo and president of the Privy Council (and mouthpiece of the emperor) Baron Yoshimichi Hara looked on from their seats at long, silk-covered conference tables. At the same tables were the chiefs of staff from the army and navy, the minister of finance, the president of the Planning Board, and the other men who would determine Japan's future course of action.

Everyone in attendance knew they were participating in an elaborate charade intended to confer legitimacy upon a decision that had already been reached. The Imperial Council's true job was rubber-stamping the findings of a conference staged the previous day between the army and navy's top leaders.

Tojo wasted little time getting to the point. "We have come to the conclusion that we must now decide to go to war, set

LEFT | General Hideki Tojo became prime minister of Japan in October of 1941. Emperor Hirohito urged him to find a peaceful resolution to the crisis. When that failed, he became a forceful advocate of a surprise attack.

65

the time for military action at the beginning of December, concentrate all of our efforts on completing preparations for war, and at the same time try to break the impasse by means of diplomacy," he told the assembly. Talks with the United States would continue even though there was almost no chance of a breakthrough.

Although Tojo dare not reveal the secret, a group of Japanese bombers had staged a rehearsal of Operation Hawaii earlier that day. It was for the most part a great success, with one exception: commanders wanted the horizontal bombers to be more accurate.

Foreign Minister Togo reinforced Tojo's opinion. "The prospects of achieving an amicable settlement in the negotiations are, to our deepest regret, dim," he said. Togo explained that Japan sought peace and stability in East Asia and had shown "patience and a spirit of compromise" in its negotiations with the United States, yet "the American Government . . . maintained an extremely firm attitude." The Americans were assisting Chiang Kai-shek's Nationalist government in China, imposing harsh economic sanctions on Japan, and supplying the Soviet Union with supplies for use in its war against Hitler—a sure sign of the Roosevelt administration's hostility toward the Axis alliance of Japan, Germany, and Italy. "Our Empire must be prepared to sweep away any and all obstacles," Togo declared.

Hirohito eyed the proceedings as momentum for action built. "We are prepared for war," Navy Chief of Staff Osami Nagano asserted. "We will take all possible measures to be ready to use force at the beginning of December," seconded Army Chief of Staff Hajime Sugiyama. One speaker after another emphasized the need for speed. Delays would give the Americans time to improve their defenses and churn out more weapons. Postponing an offensive beyond early December would also increase the chances of encountering bad weather. And each passing day saw Japan's oil reserves decline just a little bit lower.

ABOVE | Shigenori Togo served as Japan's ambassador to Germany and the Soviet Union in the late 1930s before becoming foreign minister. He opposed war with the United States.

Finally Baron Hara rose to speak, which really meant that the emperor was speaking. The baron asked a few pointed questions without ever challenging the basic premise of the discussion. Tojo confirmed the United States' intractability on the China issue. Sugiyama assured him that the conquest of South Asia would take five months and that neither the Americans nor the Soviets were likely to offer much opposition.

With these matters resolved and on the official record, Hara summarized the situation. Japan would make one last diplomatic pitch, albeit one that offered nothing new of consequence. Should that fail, as it likely would, the first blow would land in early December. "If we miss the present opportunity to go to war," he said, "we will have to submit to American dictation. Therefore, I recognize that it is inevitable that we must decide to start a war against the United States . . . if Japan is to survive."

While the Japanese government was expressing resolute unanimity, the American government was speaking out of both sides of its mouth. The State Department, normally a relative haven for pacifists, decided that

ABOVE | The Meiji Palace in Tokyo hosted the conferences that formalized the decision to proceed with Operation Hawaii.

General Tojo's ascension represented a victory for Japanese hardliners. On the day Hirohito elevated Tojo to prime minister, a State Department memo alerted bases in the Pacific that "BEST INTELLIGENCE SUGGESTS JAPAN MIGHT ATTACK RUSSIA OR BRITISH AND DUTCH COLONIES IN THE EAST INDIES."

The War Department viewed the situation differently. Though aware of the danger, it was advocating a cautious approach toward Japan. Hours before the Imperial Council reached its decision, a joint Army-Navy board concluded that "war between the United States and Japan should be avoided" even if Japan launched new offensives. American involvement in Asia would divert resources from a potential showdown with Hitler, who both the military and Roosevelt saw as the greater threat.

General George Marshall and Admiral Harold Stark made their position clear to the president in a note sent on November 5. "At the present time the United States Fleet in the Pacific is inferior to the Japanese Fleet and cannot undertake an unlimited strategic offensive in the Western Pacific," they wrote. Military necessity demanded the maintenance of peace for as long as possible.

But peace at what price? On November 7, Japan's ambassador to the United States, Kichisaburo Nomura, presented Secretary of State Cordell Hull with what was clearly his government's final offer. Hull saw nothing "fundamentally new" in the document. Japan tendered a vague plan to withdraw troops from China sometime after the war there had ended. Hull was aware of the proposals even before the meeting, having read secret decryptions of Japan's diplomatic chatter. After reading the memos, Roosevelt advised his secretary of state to "do nothing to precipitate a crisis." At a cabinet meeting later that afternoon, Hull warned that "relations were extremely critical and that we should be on the lookout for a military attack anywhere by Japan at any time."

"Things seem to be moving steadily toward a crisis in the Pacific," Admiral Stark wrote Admiral Husband Kimmel that same day.

ABOVE | Franklin D. Roosevelt and Winston Churchill's secret August 1941 meeting off the coast of Newfoundland produced the Atlantic Charter, a statement of shared war aims. It also reflected the tightening relationship between the two countries.

Cordell Hull and Kichisaburo Nomura had known each other for a short time, yet their relationship pretty accurately mirrored the larger US-Japan relationship. Though by no means friends, they shared a common respect and a desire to get along with each other. At the same time, neither of these diplomats could ever shake his cultural prejudices enough to actually comprehend the political and cultural position of his counterpart. Each upheld his nation's interests with stubborn inflexibility while hoping they could somehow avoid a fight that was assuming an air of inevitability.

Hull was born in a log cabin in Tennessee and had spent decades as a judge, a state legislator, and a congressman before accepting FDR's nomination as Secretary of State. Roosevelt respected Hull as an elder statesman but was never personally close with him and often kept him out of the loop on important matters. Hull sometimes referred to the president as "that man across the street who never tells me anything."

The secretary was a blunt and direct man with no time for witty phrasings or clever allusions. His silver hair, high forehead, and skeptical expression gave him a permanently serious demeanor not even his curiously high-pitched voice could diminish. He was dull and predictable, thorough and hard working. Washington's social scene meant nothing to him. Croquet was his sport of choice.

Hull's advocacy of free trade had guided his perspective toward Japan for many years. The secretary believed that open markets increased trade and encouraged global stability. He opposed economic sanctions against Japan on the grounds that they would simply force the empire to seek resources elsewhere, thereby increasing the chances of war. Hull therefore disapproved of the administration's ever-lengthening list of embargoed trade items but could not muster enough bureaucratic influence to reverse the tide.

Hull accepted Nomura's diplomatic credentials in February 1941. Nomura had not

ABOVE | Secretary of State Cordell Hull often felt isolated in President Roosevelt's cabinet. An idealist and an advocate of free trade, he was also a tough negotiator with the Japanese.

ABOVE | Cordell Hull (center) met several times with Ambassador Kichisaburo Nomura (left) and special envoy Saburo Kurusu in the weeks prior to the attack on Pearl Harbor. Despite their mutual respect, their talks were bound to fail.

wanted the ambassador position. A former admiral and foreign minister, he was sixty-two years old and living in comfortable semi-retirement before getting pressed back into national service. His well-known soft spot for Americans and acquaintance with President Roosevelt, a fellow naval aficionado, made him the ideal person for the job.

Nomura met with Hull around four dozen times in 1941, often in the secretary's apartment in the Carlton Hotel. Although they maintained a fairly easy rapport, Nomura labored under a series of burdens that made it nearly impossible to achieve any diplomatic breakthroughs.

Language was a constant barrier. Nomura spoke passable English—certainly better than Hull's nonexistent Japanese—but often understood only the gist of the secretary's conversation. Detail and nuance escaped him, as it would with most nonnative speakers. Only rarely would he use a translator.

Nomura was also hamstrung by his government's opaque nature. Often he had no idea what his superiors were thinking or what secret plans were afoot in Tokyo. More

ABOVE | Japan's government gave Ambassador Nomura (right) an impossible assignment: broker peace with Secretary of State Hull (left) without conceding any of Japan's vital interests.

than once he had to apologize for telling Hull something that later proved untrue. On those occasions he would beg for patience and understanding, explaining that "there was politics in the situation back in Japan." Evidence indicates that Nomura was ignorant of Operation Hawaii and did not know the decision for war had essentially been made by November 1941.

In fact, Hull often knew more about what was happening in Japan than Nomura, because the secretary was reading the top-secret Magic decryptions of the empire's diplomatic codes. Hull knew Nomura's proposals before the ambassador even entered the room. He also knew when his counterpart was making an argument that did not match up with reality.

It slowly became clear that the two diplomats were fighting a delaying action rather than actually heading off a war. Positions

had calcified with no hope for compromise. The Roosevelt administration insisted that the United States would offer concessions only after Japan left China. Japanese officials ordered Nomura to reply that Japan would leave China once the United States offered concessions. No one was budging.

Nomura desperately wanted to end his mission and go home. Instead, in the wake of the Imperial Council's November 5 meeting, Tokyo dispatched a reinforcement in the person of Saburo Kurusu, an experienced diplomat with an American wife and a solid understanding of the United States, having lived in Chicago for six years in the 1910s. His superiors did not know he privately opposed both Japan's involvement in the Axis and a war with the United States.

Tojo handed Kurusu a nearly impossible assignment. "Be sure to give it your best effort and come to an agreement," the prime minister advised him before adding that "Japan could not possibly concede on the point of troop withdrawal." Kurusu needed to somehow force the United States to back down without offering his counterparts anything new. Tojo put the odds of success at 30 percent. Kurusu thought that figure optimistic.

Hull accompanied Nomura and Kurusu to the White House on November 17 for an 11:00 a.m. conference with Roosevelt. As

ABOVE | In 1941, Japan's government gave Saburu Kurusu the most difficult assignment of his thirty-year career as a diplomat: broker peace with the United States without conceding any of Japan's interests in Asia.

72

everyone exchanged pleasantries, FDR sized up his new visitor and found him lacking. Kurusu was cold and excessively formal, precisely attired and impeccably mannered. In other words, he was everything that Roosevelt was not. More important, as they spoke, the president felt their conversation only repeated what had already been said. There was no movement on the China question despite Kurusu's repeated statements that the two sides must reach an amicable agreement. Nor would Kurusu renounce the Axis pact, as Roosevelt and Hull demanded. Japan's diplomatic ties with Germany only added to the empire's toxicity. Ever the optimist, FDR ended the conference on an upbeat note, remarking as his guests exited that "there is no last word between friends."

Nomura and Kurusu recognized their current negotiating stance was going nowhere. Time was ticking away. Tojo had given them until November 25 to reach an agreement. The Japanese government extended the deadline to November 29, warning that "after that things are automatically going to happen."

The pair interrupted Hull's Thanksgiving—Thursday, November 20—so they could present a second option, known as Plan B or Proposal B. Nomura indicated that this was their last gambit, "absolutely final."

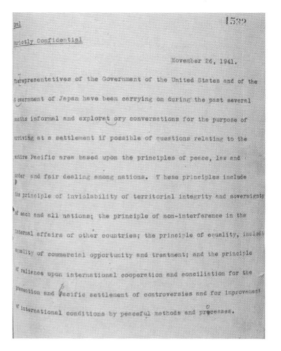

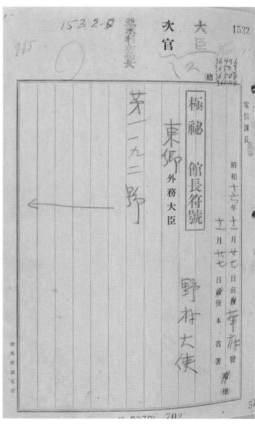

ABOVE | (Top) "This is an ultimatum," Prime Minister Tojo said when he read the so-called Hull Note of November 1941, which represented the United States' final peace offer. (Bottom) A Japanese translation of the Hull Note.

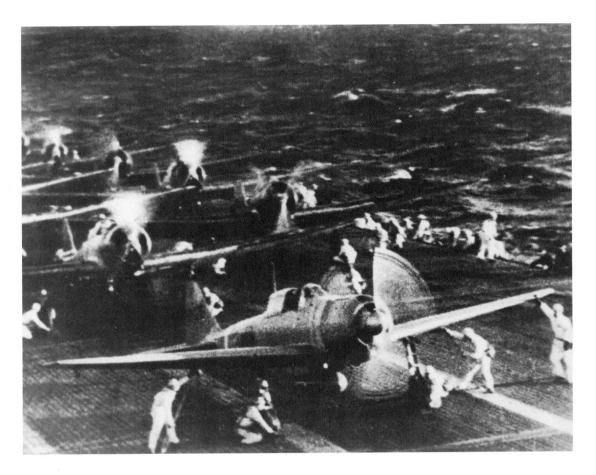

Hull made a show of reading the document, never letting on that he had already seen a copy courtesy of Magic. Ushering out his guests, he promised to give Plan B "sympathetic study." According to notes taken by Hull's aide, Joseph Ballantine, "No time was set for the next meeting."

In essence, Plan B would have kept Japanese troops in China. The United States would lift its trade restrictions in exchange for a Japanese retreat from the northern part of Indochina and a promise not to invade the rest of Southeast Asia. According to Hull, signing off on this meant "condonement by the United States of Japan's past aggressions, assent by the United States to unlimited courses of conquest by Japan in the future, [and] abandonment by the United States of its whole past position in regard to the most essential principles of its foreign policy in general."

Japan's navy was gearing up for action even as the unfortunate Nomura and Kurusu were making offers they knew the United States would refuse. As much as Admiral Yamamoto dreaded war, it was time to set the Hawaii plan into motion. Fighters and bombers

ABOVE | Japanese Mitsubishi dive-bombers warm up on the deck of a carrier before heading toward Pearl Harbor.

74

began leaving their bases for the aircraft carriers, and the fleet practiced refueling procedures. Naval radiomen disguised the location of the fleet with a cloud of phony broadcasts. Tokyo asked its confidants on Oahu for more frequent updates detailing which ships were anchored in Pearl Harbor. Washington picked up enough of this chatter through Magic to recognize that something was happening. Just what it was remained unclear.

Roosevelt was still looking for a way out of the showdown, or at least a way to delay the inevitable. During a meeting with Hull, he scribbled an outline of a temporary arrangement, or modus vivendi, between the two countries. The proposed deal would last six months, during which time the United States would resume some shipments of oil and rice and back away from talks between Japan and China. In exchange, Japan would pledge not to commit additional troops to the front or to invoke its Axis obligations should the United States enter the war in Europe.

In remaining silent on the China issue, Roosevelt was offering a major concession. As with anything involving FDR, his exact thoughts were unclear; he loved launching test balloons. At times he governed by confusion, casting out ideas just to see how people responded, or to see whether someone offered a better idea. FDR often said one thing to one aide, then the complete opposite to the next person he saw.

Responses to the modus vivendi proposal, if it truly was a proposal and not a musing, were mixed. Hull was willing to give it a chance. Other cabinet members, including Treasury Secretary Henry Morgenthau and Secretary of War Henry Stimson, were outraged at the thought of weakening the United States' posture. Chiang Kai-shek made his displeasure clear as well, arguing that any suspension of American aid to China would doom his embattled government.

ABOVE | Chinese political and military leader Chiang Kai-shek encouraged the United States to focus its power on Japan, which had invaded his country in 1931 and 1937, rather than on Germany.

Roosevelt also sought input from a man who was quickly becoming one of his closest advisors: British prime minister Winston Churchill. The two had engaged in a spirited correspondence ever since Churchill's elevation in mid-1940. Churchill found the president charming if a bit glib. Roosevelt found the prime minister determined if long-winded. They were two alpha dogs who were used to being the center of attention but nevertheless made room for each other in their respective kennels. Their relationship was founded on personal affection and mutual interest. Roosevelt needed Britain to survive its war against Hitler, and Churchill needed the United States to help his country as much as possible.

The modus vivendi "seems to me a fair proposition for the Japanese but its acceptance or rejection is really a matter of internal Japanese politics," Roosevelt wrote in a cable to the "Former Naval Person," as he called Churchill. "I am not very hopeful and we must all be prepared for real trouble, possibly soon," he concluded. The prime minister shared FDR's doubts. "Our anxiety is about China," he responded. "If they collapse, our joint dangers would enormously increase." There was no need for stating the obvious. If China was overrun, the United States would have to divert resources from the European theater,

something Churchill could not bear. Losing China would also leave Britain's colonies in Asia even more vulnerable to Japanese attack.

In a follow-up cable, Churchill urged a stronger approach. Rather than broker a deal, the president should make "a plain declaration . . . that any further act of aggression by Japan will lead immediately to the gravest consequences."

Roosevelt preferred nebulous language that permitted maximum flexibility of action rather than rhetorical lines in the sand. Even so, his back had already stiffened by the time Churchill sent his bracing message. The turning point came on November 26 when Secretary Stimson brought the president an update on Japanese activities in the Pacific. A fleet of thirty to fifty ships had been sighted off the coast of Taiwan. It was heading south, toward Indochina, with five divisions on board. FDR "fairly blew up," Stimson wrote. Anyone could see what was going on. The Japanese were staging sham negotiations as cover for an impending offensive.

This revelation killed whatever chance the modus vivendi had. Roosevelt ordered Hull to reject Japan's Plan B. On November 26 the secretary gave Nomura and Kurusu two memos, known collectively as the Hull Note, that sounded a lot like an ultimatum. The Note reiterated such basic principles as

international cooperation and equal access to trade markets while demanding that Japan withdraw from China and Indochina. Hull deflected the diplomats' complaints while holding out the possibility that Roosevelt might grant them another meeting.

As Hull indicated, the door to an agreement was closing but not yet shut. In a cable to Tokyo, Nomura and Kurusu suggested a high-level summit, perhaps between former Prime Minister Fumimaro Konoe and Vice President Henry Wallace. Tokyo, however,

ABOVE | With Great Britain fighting for its existence against Germany, Prime Minister Winston Churchill urged President Roosevelt to establish a strong presence in both the Atlantic and the Pacific Oceans.

saw no point in more talking. Prime Minister Tojo decided that the United States was "unyielding and unbending." On December 1 Nomura received orders to destroy the embassy's code machine and burn its codes.

Nomura received a cable from Foreign Minister Togo on December 6. "The Government has deliberated deeply on the American proposal of the 26th of November," it read, speaking of the Hull Note, "and as a result we have drawn up a memorandum for the United States." The message would be "very long," Togo warned, consisting of fourteen parts, and would arrive soon. "Put it in nicely drafted form and make every preparation to present it to the Americans just as soon as you receive instructions," the cable concluded.

On that same day, December 6, Roosevelt attempted one last maneuver. One-to-one communication had always been his strong suit. He saw a chance—a slim one—that a personal message to Hirohito might head off a war.

FDR delivered a call for reason, not a new proposal. "Only in situations of extraordinary importance to our two countries need I address to Your Majesty messages on matters of state," his letter opened. "I feel I should now so address you because of the deep and far-reaching emergency which appears to be in formation." Roosevelt briefly reviewed the crisis in China and lamented Japan's thrust toward Southeast Asia. "It is clear that a continuance of such a situation is unthinkable," he said, striking a tone somewhere between resolute and regretful. Roosevelt made no promises beyond assuring the emperor that the United States would not invade Indochina if Japan pulled out.

"I address myself to Your Majesty at this moment in the fervent hope that Your Majesty may, as I am doing, give thought in this definite emergency to ways of dispelling the dark clouds," Roosevelt concluded. "I am confident that both of us, for the sake of the peoples not only of our own great countries but for the sake of humanity in neighboring territories, have a sacred duty to restore traditional amity and prevent further death and destruction in the world."

Roosevelt felt he could do no more. At 9:00 p.m. he dispatched the telegram to Ambassador Joseph Grew in Tokyo along with orders to give it to Hirohito as soon as possible. "Well," FDR sighed, "this son of man has just sent his final message to the son of God."

We Salute the
CHINESE REPUBLIC
On her Birthday OCTOBER 10TH

China - the First of our Allies to fight Japan,
China - in spite of war, struggling victoriously
toward Democracy as we did 150 years ago.

HELP HER TO FIGHT BRAVELY ON!

UNITED CHINA RELIEF
Member Agency of the National War Fund

ABOVE | Americans had stereotyped the Chinese as "good Asians" years before Pearl Harbor. China sought American aid in its war against Japan.

CHAPTER 5
AT THE THRESHOLD OF GLORY OR OBLIVION

The spot was fitting. The Kurile Islands stretch from northern Japan to Russia's Kamchatka Peninsula like an extended chain. It is part of the Pacific Ocean's Ring of Fire—volcanic islands on top of an unstable tectonic plate that threatens to erupt with destructive force. The Kurile's weather is as harsh as its geology. Winters stretch on seemingly forever—a nightmare of long dark nights and high winds that bring driving snowstorms. In the summers come the fog, thick and wet and inhospitable. It's hardly surprising that the islands are best remembered for their military history. A Japanese warlord used the chain as a forward base to invade Kamchatka in the Russo-Japanese War of 1904–1905, and in 1918 a Japanese military expedition, allied with British and American forces, moved into Russia in a failed attempt to influence the outcome of the Russian Civil War.

In November 1941, the Kurile Islands once again served as a gathering point for a hostile force. Throughout the last part of the

LEFT | The flagship of the Pearl Harbor Strike Force was the carrier *Akagi*. Like the *Kaga*, it did not survive the Battle of Midway in June 1942.

month, Japanese warships had chugged into the North Pacific bound for Hitokappu Bay on Iturup Island. The deepwater port was a perfect rendezvous spot, shrouded by fog and virtually uninhabited except for naval personnel. Away from the prying eyes of foreigners the ships slipped into place. One after another they came, a strike force to be reckoned with—six aircraft carriers, two battleships, two heavy cruisers, one light cruiser, and nine destroyers, as well as submarines and tankers. With thirty-two ships in all, and over four hundred aircrafts, the armada was one of the most awesome forces in the history of naval warfare.

Aboard the flagship carrier *Akagi* sat the First Air Fleet's commander, Vice Admiral Chuichi Nagumo. Thick and powerful through the chest and shoulders, with the chin and jaw of a boxer, Nagumo looked like a warrior. And he was. Although he had performed admirably in a number of shore jobs, it was sea service that he craved, and fellow officers claimed he really was at ease only when his ship was skipping over waves. Sea duty meant the likelihood of battle and the chance to sacrifice his life for the emperor, and those were possibilities that he embraced.

It was this love affair with death in defense of country that Nagumo shared with so many other graduates of Etajima, Japan's naval academy. The school, tucked behind a mountain on an island in the Inland Sea, was a beautiful place, but it was also terrible.

ABOVE | US bombers on a windswept Aleutian air base prepare to attack the Japanese in the Kurile Islands. Both places share an inhospitable climate.

Young cadets were punched in the face if they saluted improperly, forced to stand for hours in the sun for the slightest infraction, and systematically broken down physically and mentally. "After a few months of such treatment, the newcomers became sheep-like in their obedience," wrote a graduate. They became the clay out of which fanatical, and often brutal, officers were molded. As the academy's song proclaimed, "Our hearts throb more and more with the hot blood / Of the Sons of the Sacred Land / We shall never stop sacrificing ourselves."

The grim life at Etajima turned graduates into fatalistic men. "Whatever is to be will be," one wrote in his diary on his way to battle. But Nagumo lacked such extreme fatalism. In a photograph taken in his full dress uniform, his face looks strong and resolved, save for his eyes. There is a sadness in them, the haunted look of a man who might be crushed under the burden of command. The strike fleet in Hitokappu Bay was his to lead, but his orders called for an attack into the very heart of the enemy's strength. The audacious assault might bring glory and military immortality. Or it could end in disaster and ignominy.

Any act of fate might befall Nagumo. If the weather was clear and the seas calm, some ship might see his fleet and radio its position. Or the fleet might be separated by a storm.

ABOVE | Aircraft on the *Akagi* prepare to launch a second wave toward Pearl Harbor and destiny.

Yamamoto was fond of the proverb that said if you wanted the tiger's cubs you had to venture into the tiger's lair. But what would happen if the tiger discovered you before you were in position to strike? The gamble weighed heavily on Nagumo.

Nagumo was a questionable leader of the Pearl Harbor attack for more reasons than his temperament. His previous command experience was wrong for the mission. During his long, distinguished career, he had served on and commanded battleships, cruisers, and destroyers. He understood the advantages of submarines and the tactics of battleship warfare. But the future belonged to aircraft carriers—and he belonged to the past. Nagumo, as one of his friends explained, "was wholly unfitted by background, training, experience, and interest for a major role in Japan's naval air arm. He had no conception of the real power and potentialities of the air arm when he became Commander in Chief of the First Air Fleet."

The local time was 0600 on November 26—1030 November 25 in Honolulu and 1600 November 25 in Washington, DC—when the engines of *Akagi* began to stir and the orders to hoist the anchor were given. Dark, low clouds seemed to reach to the sea, and snow fell into the cold, inky waters. Soon *Akagi* slipped out of the bay into the Pacific Ocean, and the other ships assumed their specified positions. They were on their way.

The sailors and pilots aboard the ships breathed in the freezing Pacific air, some looking back toward the land, others out into the sea. Like Nagumo, they, too, were warriors, determined to perform their duties and stoically accept their fates. "For most of the members of the task force," historian Gordon W. Prange wrote, "the whole problem boiled down to what the grim business of war had been for all men in all ages: Kill or be killed." Captain Takahisa Amagai captured the fatalism of the men, commenting that once they left the Kuriles "the young officers simply did not give a damn what happened."

Gales pounded the ships, fog hid one from another. Navigation officers worked to keep the vessels in their proper positions. In the center the carriers formed two, three-ship columns. The battleships and cruisers guarded their flanks, and the destroyers screened the entire force. Submarines scouted out in front, and tankers bobbed along in the rear. Mostly their formation was standard. But because of the poor visibility, a strict blackout, and radio silence, Nagumo pulled his submarines closer to the other ships. He worried that if the subs got too far out in front they might lose contact with the main fleet. Of course, by pulling them back he limited the range of his forward eyes, risking a possible chance encounter with another ship.

While the forward visibility was limited by his submarine placement, his communications with the rear were virtually nonexistent. The normal radio chatter from ship to ship and back to home base had been scuttled to maintain mission secrecy. Lonely in command, the silence tortured Nagumo. Although he was supposed to get the final "Stop" or "Go" command from the authorities in Tokyo by way of a predetermined wavelength, he fretted about some sort of unforeseen malfunction. He might miss the message. Or there could be a system failure.

As the First Air Fleet sailed across the

North Pacific—a route designed to avoid the most trafficked sea lanes—Nagumo had time enough to manufacture a wide assortment of possible complications. He took every precaution to avoid detection. He ordered that no waste be tossed overboard to avoid a human footprint, that used oil drums be stored in the hold, and that the fleet use a cleaner-burning fuel. But still he worried. He agonized that the tankers' thicker black smoke would draw the attention of some distant ship—an unlikely scenario. He feared that an enemy submarine would spot the fleet—equally unlikely given the

ABOVE | The *Akagi*'s guns were formidable. Twin 120mm, .45-caliber antiaircraft guns protected the port side.

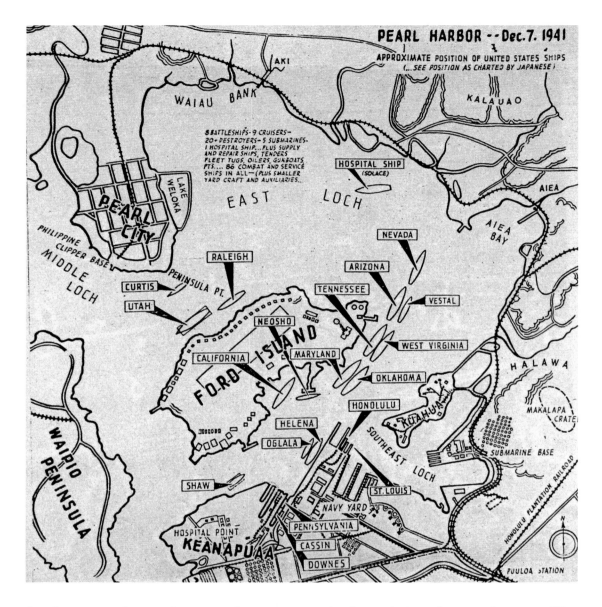

few American subs anywhere near the area and the immensity of the North Pacific. He stressed over the problems of refueling in the roiling seas—but he enjoyed an unusual stretch of calm seas. And on top of it all was his dread of missing the signal.

Nagumo's face reflected his concerns, and several officers on *Akagi* became alarmed that he might give the crew the jitters. "Yes, the operation is big," his chief of staff told him, "but now that we are under way there is no use to worry. The only logical thing to do is to carry on fearlessly."

While Nagumo faced his demons, his leading crew members prepared for the attack. Commander Mitsuo Fuchida, the

ABOVE | In the wake of the attack, Americans scrambled for any information about Pearl Harbor and the surrounding areas. Japan, of course, had far more detailed knowledge of the port.

commander of all the air groups of the First Air Fleet, displayed a philosophical calm. Throughout the voyage across the Pacific his pilots and crews occupied their days checking out their planes; studying photographs of American aircraft carriers, battleships, cruisers, and destroyers; and memorizing the geography of Oahu and the various American airfields and bases. At night they played games, drank *sake*, and enjoyed the brotherhood of warriors. "They did not fear death," Fuchida later remarked. "Their only fear was that the attack might not be successful and that they would have to return to Japan with their mission unfulfilled."

Commander Minoru Genda buried his concerns in work, constructing contingency plans on top of contingency plans. Looking in the mirror he noticed white hairs around his temple. He attributed their appearance to work and worry. His greatest concern was Nagumo. Unlike the vice admiral, Genda was a proponent of air power, and he thought his job was to convince his commander of the necessity to bomb Pearl Harbor until Japanese pilots destroyed the American ships and the capacity of the base to make war. To accomplish this mission, Genda thought, would require Nagumo to abandon his "one attack only" mantra and order multiple air

ABOVE | The submarine base in Oahu. The supply depot is beyond and the fuel farm to the right. For the Japanese, it was a secondary target.

assaults against Pearl Harbor. Methodically, Genda devised four new plans. If the first two-wave attack succeeded, all four plans called for Nagumo to "exploit whatever situation arose."

Specifically, Genda wrote, "This might call for aerial searches to find and destroy US units not at Pearl Harbor. Or deliver repeated attacks against the remaining ships in Pearl Harbor as well as its installations." Only after Pearl Harbor lay in rubble and the US fleet had settled on the ocean floor should the First Air Fleet return to Japan.

While Nagumo fretted, Fuchida prepared, and Genda planned, back in Japan Premier Hideki Tojo and his cabinet were making the final, fateful decision to go to war with the United States. The negotiations

with America had stalled primarily because of Japan's hard stand on its occupation of much of the Chinese coast and its "special interests" in Indochina. Although Japan wanted a resumption of full trade with the United States—and especially access to American oil—it was not about to withdraw from China or scuttle its imperialistic "Greater East Asia Co-Prosperity Sphere," which is exactly what the United States demanded. It was as if the two nations were singularly mismatched dance partners. Both wanted to lead; neither would follow. And so they stumbled around the diplomatic dance floor, squandering any chance to preserve peace.

By the end of November both nations had grown weary. Nagumo's fleet was in the water steaming toward Pearl Harbor. In Tokyo war plans had replaced diplomacy. And American intercepts of Japanese diplomatic communications alerted the United States that hostilities were imminent. Japan, the Roosevelt administration's war leaders knew, was about to strike.

Even the thinnest hope for peace ended on December 1, 1941, in Tokyo when the Imperial Council voted to go to war with the United States. Premier Tojo listened as the members of the council rehashed the failure of diplomacy and the necessity of action. Finally, after the others had had their say, he

ABOVE | Prime Minister Hideki Tojo advocated the alliance with Germany and Italy and war against the United States. Loyal to the army, he lacked a keen grasp of geopolitics.

spoke. "The Razor," as he was known for his sharp decisive mind, did not mince words. The Japanese government was "fully prepared for a long war," he said, but "[we] would also like to do everything we can in the future to bring the war to an early conclusion." He felt that the stakes could not be higher: "At this moment our Empire stands at the threshold of glory or oblivion."

His Imperial Majesty Hirohito, Emperor of Japan, sat nearly motionless, nodding his head occasionally to something that was said. An observer noted that the emperor seemed in an "excellent mood" and "displayed no signs of uneasiness." He didn't contribute to the discussions, didn't voice approval or disapproval. Yet in silence he gave his consent. In truth, the decision was less a decision than a final recognition of a fait accompli. The chain of events had begun years before. It was at the core of Japanese aggressive expansionist foreign policy, expressed in its wars with China and Russia, underlying its understanding of the Greater East Asia Co-Prosperity Sphere and its ambitious plans to attack Pearl Harbor. Japan, like Hitler's Germany, seemed determined to go to war. Its conflict with the United States seemed as inevitable as Germany's with the Soviet Union.

Nagumo was halfway to Hawaii when the Imperial Council made its decision on December 2. But he soon learned of its verdict. Admiral Yamamoto's message was radioed to the First Air Fleet, and the rest of the combined fleet: *"Niitaka yama nobore ichi-ni-rei-ya."* Climb Mount Niitaka, 1208. The message signified that the attack would begin at midnight December 8 Japanese time. At just under thirteen thousand feet, Mount Niitaka in Formosa was the highest mountain in the Japanese Empire, so the coded message carried a symbolic significance. In effect, it indicated that Japan was about to reach the height of its glory. The empire was on the verge of realizing its destiny. And it would begin with Pearl Harbor.

The message was top secret, of course, but in Tokyo rumors that Japan was about to go to war had long masqueraded as established facts. Joseph Grew had already warned the State Department that Japan might launch the war with "dramatic and dangerous suddenness." He knew that the Japanese modus operandi for starting a war was to fire first and deal with the diplomatic niceties later. Japan's conflicts against China in 1894 and Russia in 1904 had begun without a formal declaration of hostilities, and Grew counseled vigilance by his government.

In Honolulu, Admiral Husband E. Kimmel, the commander of the Pacific Fleet, was also concerned. At his December 2 discussion

As the intelligence officer explained, it was very difficult to track ships working under sealed orders and preserving radio silence. And after some discussion Kimmel dropped the subject. He knew that changing radio frequencies and code burning was standard operating procedure. To be sure, he expected an eventual Japanese attack on some US holding in the Pacific—but not on Pearl Harbor. His sarcasm aside, he most assuredly did not expect a Japanese carrier fleet to round Diamond Head.

Out in the North Pacific, still hundreds of miles away, Nagumo had made his turn and was heading south by southeast toward Pearl Harbor. His fleet plowed through rough seas, sometimes rolling as much as forty-five degrees to one side and forcing the abandonment of any refueling efforts. But with his orders to "proceed with the attack," he grimly prepared for war. On December 4, the same day that his fleet crossed the international date line, he issued instructions that if an enemy or third party's warship was sighted, "her communication equipment will be destroyed if and when necessary to protect secrecy of our intension, and, in case of emergency, she will be sunk." If Nagumo could help it, nothing would be left to chance.

of intelligence reports he learned that Japan had changed its radio frequencies. The essence of the information was that Tokyo was preparing for "operations on a large scale." Alarmed, Kimmel asked for the location of Japan's aircraft carriers. His intelligence officer gave locations for all save four carriers.

"What!" Kimmel exclaimed. "You don't know where [they] are?"

"No, sir, I do not. I think they are in home waters, but—"

Cutting the man short, Kimmel responded, "Do you mean to say they could be rounding Diamond Head and you wouldn't know it?"

Fuchida's pilots felt the same way. More than ever they pored over details of Pearl

Harbor and the ships they expected to be in the port. Intelligence from Honolulu, relayed to Imperial Naval Headquarters in Tokyo and passed on to the First Air Fleet by radio, indicated that six of the US battle fleet—*Pennsylvania*, *Arizona*, *California*, *Tennessee*, *Maryland*, and *West Virginia*—were in port. The pilots wanted exact locations. Now that their mission was close, they greedily absorbed all the information they could gather, studying and restudying the charts of Pearl Harbor.

With the success of the mission dependent on them, the pilots were pampered by the crew. The flyers received daily baths, and special diets, which included eggs and milk. Cooks converted the dairy items into "American milkshakes." And so, with only a couple of days remaining before the attack, they ate and studied, repeatedly checked the engines of their planes, and dreamed of success and glory.

On December 5, the fleet refueled for the final time before the attacks. It took most of the day and night. After it was done the slow-moving tankers dropped out of the attack force and the fleet increased its speed, churning southward at twenty-four knots.

Most Americans were sound asleep by 7:00 p.m. Hawaiian time on December 6, 1941, when counterintelligence officer Lieutenant Colonel George Bicknell huddled

with Lieutenant Colonel Kendall Fielder and Lieutenant General Walter Short on Short's porch, poring over a message that might or might not tip them off to Japan's intentions. Commander of the Army forces at Pearl Harbor, Short, like Kimmel, was expecting a Japanese move, though not one toward his home base. But the latest report was disturbing.

FBI agents had forwarded a translation of a phone call between a newspaper reporter in Tokyo and a local resident, Mrs. Motokazu Mori, the wife of a Honolulu dentist. The three officers could not agree whether the intercepted conversation was portentous or mundane. "Are airplanes flying daily?" Mrs. Mori was asked. "Yes," she replied. "Lots of them fly around." From there the

conversation wandered as they discussed the weather, Japanese-American relations, and the sailors on Oahu.

"What kind of flowers are in bloom in Hawaii at present?" the reporter inquired.

"Presently, the flowers in bloom are fewest out of the whole year," replied Mori. "However, the hibiscus and the poinsettia are in bloom now."

Bicknell, Fielder, and Short dissected that last statement. On the one hand, it was true; hibiscus and poinsettia plants were blooming. On the other hand, why would anyone waste time talking about flowers during an expensive, trans-Pacific call? For an hour they parsed the document. Clearly something was up. Japanese diplomats were burning their codes. The Japanese fleet kept changing its radio call signs. Naval Intelligence had no idea where Japan's carriers were. Could this note explain these mysteries?

Finally they gave up on deciphering what the transcript meant, if it meant anything at all. Short and Fielder left for a dinner party. Bicknell retreated to his office to scrutinize the note some more before locking it in his safe and going home. It was "suspicious, very fishy," the men concluded, but they "couldn't make heads nor tails of it." Neither has anyone else in the years since.

ABOVE | The Japanese battleship *Nagato* was the flagship of Admiral Yamamoto during the attack on Pearl Harbor.

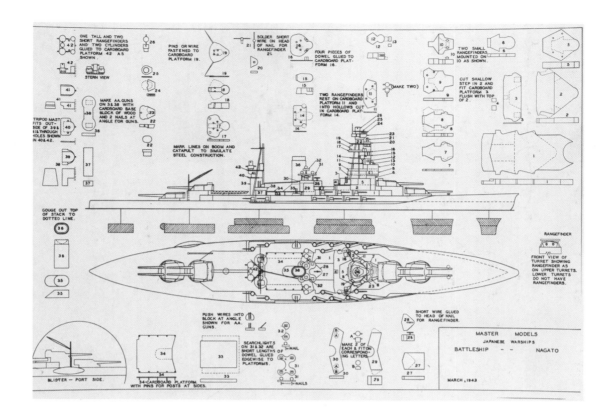

Several hundred miles to the northwest, Admiral Nagumo's fleet slashed its way through stormy seas. Cruisers, destroyers, and battleships led the armada, followed by the two columns of carriers. The four-colored Z flag that had waved above Admiral Heihachiro Togo's ship during his victory over the Russians in the 1905 Battle of Tsushima Strait now flew from the carrier *Akagi*. Cheers filled the air. A witness on the ship called it the most dramatic moment of the entire war.

As the fleet plowed its way south, pilots made their final preparations. Intelligence officers examined the latest reports from Pearl Harbor. All signs looked favorable.

More than four thousand miles away, aboard the battleship *Nagato*, Admiral Isoroku Yamamoto kept calm by playing Shogi, a Japanese version of chess. Before going to sleep, he dipped his brush in ink and composed a brief poem: "It is my sole wish to serve the Emperor as His shield / I will not spare my life or honor."

Fun, not honor, was the order of the night in Hawaii on December 6. That evening felt

ABOVE | The plans for the *Nagato*. Yamamoto was aboard, and although he was not part of the Strike Force, Pearl Harbor occupied his thoughts.

a little more festive than the usual Saturday for the officers, sailors, soldiers, and civilians who called Oahu home. Although the carriers had recently steamed out of Pearl, December 6 marked the first weekend in five months when the entire battleship fleet was in port. Old Navy pals shook hands in the clubs and showed off their new dance steps. Honolulu surged with energy as gobs swaggered into the Princess Theater to watch "Tantalizing Tootsies" and wolf whistled at Lana Turner onscreen with Clark Gable in *Honky Tonk*. Back at Pearl, the poor suckers without shore leave consoled themselves by cheering their favorites at the Fleet Band Championships. Most thought *Arizona*'s band was the best, though the judges eliminated it in an early round.

Although recent events put the base on alert, a curious mellowness pervaded the scene. The planes at Hickam and Wheeler airfields were parked in tight rows as a defense against potential saboteurs. Antiaircraft batteries sat with empty chambers; crews had locked away their ammunition, again to protect against sabotage. It was as if the base was trying to convey peaceful intentions. Even the sailors seemed unusually well behaved.

The shore patrol stopped a fight between two crewmen from *Honolulu*, and MPs hauled twenty-five people to the drunk tank at Fort Shafter, but overall the authorities enjoyed a relatively quiet evening.

Out on the Pacific Ocean, some 220 miles north of Oahu, dawn arrived with the roar of engines. As the Japanese carriers pitched four to five degrees in the six-foot swells, they began to launch their planes. Commander Fuchida was in the lead high-level bomber. He had slept soundly the night before. "I had set up the whole machinery of attack," he later remembered, "and it was ready to go. There was no use to worry now."

Fastidious in his habits, Fuchida had dressed carefully. He wore red underwear and a red shirt, so that if he were wounded in battle his blood would not show on the red cloth and demoralize his fellow pilots. As he got ready to climb into the cockpit he tied a *hachimaki* around his head. On it was a single word: *Hissho* (Certain Victory).

At about 6:20 a.m., with the first wave's 183 planes in the air, Fuchida took his own group of bombers across *Akagi*'s bow and set course for Pearl Harbor. The attack had begun.

CHAPTER 6
THIS IS NOT A DRILL

I t was 7:02 a.m. on December 7, and Private Joseph Lockard and Private George Elliott were ready for breakfast. Their three-hour shift at the mobile army radar unit at Opana, atop a hill on Oahu's northern coast, had ended two minutes earlier. The pickup truck that would take them home would be arriving at any moment.

Lockard was shutting down the unit when a spray of green blobs splashed across his screen. Something was coming from the north, something big. Whatever it was, it was around 137 miles away. Elliott suggested calling Fort Shafter's Information Center. Lockard, the more experienced of the two men, didn't want to, as their duty hours had ended.

Elliott might have been more anxious had he known that the minesweeper *Condor* had sighted a submarine outside the harbor at 3:42 a.m., or that the destroyer *Ward* had dropped depth charges on a different submarine at around 6:45 a.m. Ambiguous phrasing, along with the frequency of mistaken reports of contacts with enemy subs, prevented the news from receiving the priority it deserved.

Elliott insisted that reporting what they were seeing would provide everyone with some good practice. Lockard finally agreed.

to Oahu. Navigators used the radio signal to guide their planes to the airport.

"Don't worry about it," Tyler said. The blips were either some B-17s arriving from the mainland or navy planes launched from the carriers. He hung up.

Elliott kept watching the screen. The planes were heading for Oahu, no doubt about that. They were sixty miles away. Forty. Twenty.

Their truck arrived. Hungry, they switched off the machine, climbed into the truck, and headed off at 7:45 a.m.

Elliott got Lieutenant Kermit Tyler on the phone. Tyler was the only officer in the Information Center at the time. Everyone else had just left for breakfast. That morning was only the second time Tyler had pulled such duty.

The blips were getting closer. Taking the phone, Lockard said that they were "the biggest sightings he had ever seen."

Tyler had an answer to the mystery. On his way in that morning he had listened to Hawaiian songs playing on station KGMB. A friend of his, a bomber pilot, had once told him that the station stayed on the air at night whenever a flight of bombers was on its way

At that same moment, a delivery boy named Tadao Fuchikami was making his rounds atop a two-cylinder Indian Scout motorcycle. One of the envelopes in his bag was marked "Commanding General." The letter inside was for Lieutenant General Short at Fort Shafter. Nothing on the envelope suggested that the message was particularly important, so Fuchikami saw no reason to alter his route to get it there early. He could not have imagined that he was carrying a potentially world-changing telegram from US Army Chief of Staff General George Marshall.

Marshall had just returned to his Washington, DC, office after a long horseback ride when aides handed him the latest decryptions from Tokyo. The message was to Ambassador Nomura. It was a long one, a fourteen-point reply to the ultimatum that Secretary Hull had presented on November 26. Part 14, which had just come through, ordered Nomura to end the negotiations.

A second, shorter decrypt, this one from Foreign Minister Togo to Nomura, was even more worrying. "Will the Ambassador please submit to the United States Government (if possible to the Secretary of State) our reply to the United States at 1:00 p.m. on the 7th, your time," it read.

This request was so specific, and so unusual—Sundays were typically days of rest for diplomats—that it set off alarm bells. Marshall's staffers believed it signaled an imminent attack.

Marshall finished reading at around 11:00 a.m., or 5:30 a.m. Hawaiian time. Within about twenty minutes an urgent, coded dispatch was being radioed to army installations in Panama, the Philippines, and San Francisco. Alerting the commanders to Nomura's 1:00 p.m. deadline, Marshall wrote, "Just what significance the hour set may have we do not know, but be on the alert accordingly."

Hawaii did not receive the transmission. Unusual atmospheric conditions over the islands blocked the signal. A frustrated War Department signal officer sent the message via Western Union instead. With the radio down, it was the fastest way of sharing the news. Marshall's warning arrived in Honolulu at 7:33 a.m. local time and soon found its way into Tadao Fuchikami's satchel for delivery.

Commander Mitsuo Fuchida's plane hummed along at 9,800 feet. A wing of 182 bombers, torpedo planes, and fighters swarmed behind him. Around his head was the *hachimaki* headband the maintenance crew aboard the carrier *Agaki* had given him.

Fuchida had been in the air for around ninety minutes, and he was worried. A blanket of clouds prevented him from seeing anything below. He knew he was going in the right direction because he had his radio direction finder homed in on station KGMB. His greatest fear was that the lack of visibility had caused him to overshoot his target. Even if he hadn't, the airman feared that cloudy conditions might hamper the attack.

Fuchida gazed downward through his binoculars, straining for a glimpse of the surface. Then the music stopped so an announcer could read a weather report.

Partly cloudy, with good visibility, he said. Fuchida smiled, knowing that the sky would open at the perfect moment.

Moments later, Fuchida's plane soared through the predicted break in the clouds. Oahu stretched out below him, warm and green, looking exactly like it had in the training materials.

"*Tenkai!*" Fuchida barked, breaking radio silence. His planes deployed into attack position. Fuchida faced a split-second decision. His orders were to fire one shot from his signal pistol if he had achieved surprise, in which

case the torpedo bombers would go in first, followed by the horizontal bombers and the dive-bombers. Two shots would indicate that the enemy was expecting them, in which case the dive-bombers and fighters would focus on the island's air defenses while the torpedo planes waited for them to establish air superiority before going after the ships.

At 7:40 a.m., Fuchida fired a single shot. They had caught the enemy napping. Most of his planes responded, but some of the fighters did not. Deciding they had missed the first signal, Fuchida fired again. This time

ABOVE | The hangar area of the Naval Air Station at Oahu's Kanehoe Bay was one of the first targets hit by the attack.

100

the fighters moved into position. The other pilots believed their commander had just given the "Surprise Lost" signal. Confusion reigned as bombers, torpedo planes, and fighters simultaneously pursued two different attack plans.

Fuchida was furious at the miscue, but there was no time for restoring order. The planes were screaming toward their targets. At 7:49 a.m. he gave the signal to attack. *"To, to, to, to!"* he radioed (short for *totsugeki seyo*, meaning "charge!"). Four minutes later, as the first torpedo planes were approaching

Battleship Row, he radioed *Akagi* to let Admiral Nagumo know that surprise had been achieved.

"Tora! Tora! Tora!"

Ensign G. S. Flannigan was in his bunk aboard *Arizona* when the air-raid siren jerked him to attention. He and his mates grumbled about the obscenity of staging a drill on a Sunday morning. Seconds later, he heard an explosion.

ABOVE | Ford Island and Battleship Row, the heart of American sea power in the Pacific and the site of some of the worst carnage of December 7, 1941.

Pearl Harbor was such an unlikely target that the Americans could not grasp that they were under attack. "Hell, I didn't even know they were sore at us," one seaman on the destroyer *Monaghan* said. "They've changed the color of our planes," thirteen-year-old James Mann, Jr. thought as he watched more than a hundred fighters and bombers circling his family's beach house. "Very realistic maneuvers," commented Colonel William Farthing from his post in the control tower of Hickam Field. "I wonder what the Marines are doing to the Navy so early Sunday." Such disbelief even survived the first bomb blasts. "Boy," wondered one radioman as he watched a hangar explode, "is somebody going to catch it for putting live bombs on those planes!"

Fuchida's force divided. His dive-bombers and fighters headed for the airfields scattered around the island, while his torpedo planes passed over sugarcane and pineapple fields on their way to the harbor.

Aviation Machinist Guy C. Avery was half asleep on his sun porch when a squad of Zero fighters opened fire on the Marine Corps base at Kanehoe, about five miles west of Pearl Harbor. "The Japs are here! It's war!" he shouted. "Well, don't worry about it, Avery," replied a snoozing friend, "it'll last only two weeks."

Avery's watch read 7:48 a.m. Seven minutes later, Lieutenant Commander Logan Ramsey was investigating reports that *Ward* had sunk a Japanese submarine when a plane whizzed past the command center at Ford Island. "Get that fellow's number," he barked, "I want to report him for about sixteen violations of the course and safety regulations."

A minute later, explosions started erupting from nearby Hickam Field. At nearly the same instant, the first torpedoes slammed into the minelayer *Oglala* and the cruiser *Helena*. A few antiaircraft guns, some manned by sailors clad in pajamas, Hawaiian shirts, or swimsuits, began hammering out a reply.

Admiral Kimmel was getting dressed in his quarters while speaking on the phone with one of his commanders. A yeoman interrupted the conversation, shouting "There's a message from the signal tower saying the Japanese are attacking Pearl Harbor and this is no drill!" Kimmel, still fumbling with his jacket buttons, hung up and rushed outside to see what was happening. He watched from his neighbor's lawn as planes executed lazy figure eights over the harbor before starting their bombing runs. The admiral's face went pale when he discerned the rising sun insignias on the wings. "The sky was full of the enemy," he later said.

At 7:58 a.m., the command tower at Ford Island began broadcasting the message: "AIR RAID, PEARL HARBOR. THIS IS NOT A DRILL." Officers tried to scramble patrol planes, but a good number of the planes were already in flames. Parked wingtip to wingtip, they made easy targets for the Japanese bombers.

Kimmel watched in horror as a torpedo struck *Arizona*. The mighty battleship, weighing around thirty thousand tons even without all the men and gear on board, heaved out of the water, splashed back down, and began listing.

His car pulled up—he couldn't remember summoning it, but there it was. The situation had already worsened by the time he arrived at headquarters; a few minutes after 8:00 a.m. *California*, anchored behind *Nevada*, *Arizona*, *Tennessee*, and *Maryland* at the southern end of Battleship Row, had absorbed a few serious hits. Water was pouring into the ship through manhole covers that had been left open for an inspection planned for the next day. Rushing seawater fouled *California*'s fuel tanks and disabled its forward air compressor station, rendering some of its guns inoperable.

ABOVE | A Japanese bomb detonated in one of *Arizona*'s magazines. The resulting explosion tore through the ship and doomed much of its crew.

Oklahoma, moored alongside *Maryland*, was in desperate shape. "Who's the enemy?" one seaman yelled as two torpedoes slammed into the battleship. Like *California*, *Oklahoma* was opened up for inspection. Shells rolled across the deck as the vessel sagged to port. Antiaircraft crews discovered that their ammunition was locked up in chests. A hammer and chisel resolved that problem, but then the men discovered there was no air in the guns, so they couldn't load them anyway.

Oklahoma began its death roll. Commander Jesse Kenworthy, the senior officer on board—many of its senior officers, including its captain, were ashore—gave the order to abandon ship. The lucky sailors on deck threw themselves overboard. Below, men crowded around ladders offering access to the surface. A few crawled through exhaust shafts until the sun found their faces. As the ship's list neared sixty degrees, hundreds of men were still trapped belowdecks.

A fourth torpedo struck *Oklahoma* right around the time Kenworthy escaped over the starboard bilge. Watching from her home not far away, Mrs. John Earle, Admiral Kimmel's

ABOVE | Battleship Row was a cauldron of smoke and fire. *Arizona* (right), *West Virginia* (center), and *Oklahoma* (left) were all sunk during the attack. Crews later raised and refurbished *West Virginia*.

ABOVE | A view of the damage from a Japanese airplane early in the attack. *Oklahoma* and *Maryland* (top), *West Virginia* and *Tennessee* (center), and *Vestal* and *Arizona* (bottom) are all in peril.

neighbor, remembered the scene. "Slowly, sickeningly, the *Oklahoma* began to roll over on her side, until, finally, only her bottom could be seen," she said. "It was awful, for the great ships were dying before my eyes."

Just as the end was coming for *Oklahoma*, a buzzing swarm of planes was tormenting the wounded *Arizona*, which had defended America ever since 1916. One well-placed bomb crashed through the forecastle alongside the second turret before detonating the ship's forward magazine. A terrific fireball leapt into the sky. Some said it was five hundred feet high, others a thousand. Plumes of blood-red smoke billowed into the air. The resulting shockwave was so powerful that it blew sailors from neighboring vessels into the water. "The ship was sinking like an earthquake had struck it, and the bridge was in flames," said one ensign remembering the scene.

Circling above *Arizona*, Commander Fuchida felt his bomber shiver under the force of the blast. A combination of awe and joy washed over him. "*Terrible indeed*," he thought.

As the battle played out before him, Admiral Kimmel maintained his composure in the face of utter insanity. At 8:12 a.m., he dispatched a message to the entire Pacific Fleet, along with Secretary of the Navy Frank Knox: "Hostilities with Japan commenced with air raid on Pearl Harbor." Not long after, a casing from a .50-caliber bullet shattered a window and bounced off the admiral's chest. Kimmel picked up the shell, looked at the grease smear it had left on his white uniform jacket, and muttered, "It would have been merciful had it killed me."

Fuchida had good reason to be happy. Monitoring the situation from above, he could see that the attack was going better than anyone could have imagined. The disappearance of the American carriers was a disappointment, but one he had anticipated before taking off from *Akagi* that morning. Looking down, he knew that his superiors, from Nagumo to Yamamoto to the emperor himself, would be pleased with what his team had accomplished.

Arizona was going under. *Oklahoma* was showing its keel. *California* was easing onto the muddy ocean floor with a drifting pool of flaming oil threatening to engulf it. The battleship *Maryland* had taken a few hits, although the dying *Oklahoma*, anchored to its outside, was shielding it from torpedo blows. Fuchida could see fires aboard *Tennessee*, which had been punctured by a few bombs. At the head of the line, *Nevada* was

listing to port with a gaping hole in its bow while flaming fuel from *Arizona* washed toward it.

West Virginia, lying alongside *Tennessee*, had also taken severe damage. "What a magnificent sight!" enthused Commander Midori Matsumura after a perfectly placed torpedo sent smoke and waterspouts soaring into the air. Although neither Fuchida nor Matsumura knew it, that same hit mortally wounded *West Virginia*'s captain, Mervyn Bennion, who at that moment was lying semiconscious with a belly wound, mumbling questions about the battle, his ship, and his men.

The Americans were mounting a proud if relatively feeble defense. Sailors fought through twisted heaps of metal and smoke-filled passageways until they reached the decks of their ship, where they grabbed guns—any gun would do—and started firing back. Aboard *West Virignia*, Doris "Dorie" Miller, a black mess attendant who was also the ship's top heavyweight boxer, hauled

ABOVE | *West Virginia* mess attendant Doris "Dorie" Miller earned a Navy Cross for his heroics at Pearl Harbor. The government used his image to energize African Americans behind the war effort. He died at the Battle of Makin in 1943.

The Highest in Honor by RAE MAVIC DEMARCO

CAPTAIN
MERVYN SHARP
BENNION
U.S.N.

FOR HIS BRAVERY CAPT. BENNION WAS AWARDED THE MEDAL OF HONOR.

HE WAS BORN IN VERNON, UTAH, ON MAY 5, 1887.

AS COMMANDING OFFICER OF THE U.S.S. WEST VIRGINIA, AFTER BEING MORTALLY WOUNDED DURING THE ATTACK ON THE FLEET IN PEARL HARBOR BY THE JAPANESE FORCES ON DEC. 7, 1941, CAPTAIN BENNION EVIDENCED APPARENT CONCERN ONLY IN FIGHTING AND SAVING HIS SHIP. WHEN FIRST AID WAS GIVEN TO HIM, HE STRONGLY PROTESTED AGAINST BEING CARRIED FROM THE BRIDGE.

Captain Bennion out of harm's way before rushing off to man a .50-caliber antiaircraft machine gun. He had never trained on the weapon and was operating mostly on instinct. Two white sailors, whose quarters it had been his job to clean, urged him on. Miller kept firing until he ran out of ammunition. Then he returned to the captain, who was slowly fading from his resting place behind the conning tower. It was no longer safe there, so Miller helped carry Bennion to the navigation bridge before moving on to assist other injured crewmen. Because of his heroics, Miller became the first African American to receive the Navy Cross and became the face of subsequent government propaganda and recruiting efforts within black communities around the United States.

Similar acts of courage were happening all over Oahu. The ripples of antiaircraft fire from the ships were growing more intense. Enraged servicemen smashed open locked ammunition boxes. On board the destroyer *Monaghan*, Boatswain's Mate Thomas Donahue heaved wrenches at low-flying planes. "I can't keep throwing things at them!" he yelled while the crew sawed at padlocks. Nearby, on the oiler *Ramapo*, Commander Duncan Curry was firing a .45 pistol at any pilot who dared fly too close.

High overhead, Fuchida was barely bothered by the resistance. Beyond being frustrated by a pointless attack on the decrepit *Utah*, an aged battleship that now served as a target ship, he was feeling fantastic. A hell-storm of flames and smoke rose from the battleships, cruisers, and destroyers below him. His force's command of the skies remained unchallenged. Japanese bombers were annihilating the B-17s, P-40s, and other aircraft sitting on the ground at Hickam, Wheeler, and Ewa fields while the Japanese Zeroes strafed survivors. Wheeler was "a sea of fire," observed First Petty Officer Kazuo Muranaka. Stunned by the lack of opposition, one Japanese pilot declared that "it was more like a practice run than actual combat."

ABOVE | Captain Mervyn Bennion was a graduate of Annapolis and a career Navy Man. His dedication and courage made him one of the many heroes of Pearl Harbor.

"Damn it, those are Japs!" exclaimed Major Truman Landon. The major was already exhausted. He was in one of twelve B-17s winging from the mainland to bolster American forces in the Philippines. Hickam Field would be their first refueling stop after a grueling, fourteen-hour flight. To save weight on their long journey, they had left their ammunition behind.

"You may run into a war," General Hap Arnold had warned before they took off. "If we are going into a war, why don't we have machine guns?" Landon wondered. But machine guns were heavy, and so were the crewmen needed to man them. Stripped down as they were, the planes were coming into Oahu on fumes, flying individually rather than in formation so as to conserve precious fuel.

Landon felt relieved when he spotted a squadron of nine planes heading north from Oahu. Someone down there had sent an escort. Then he saw flashes of gunfire. These were enemy planes, something that hadn't existed the last time his feet had touched the ground. Landon yanked the control yoke, trying to lose them in the clouds. As the B-17 groaned its approval, he finally observed the red circles on his antagonists' wings.

Landon evaded his opponents and lined

ABOVE | Nearly two hundred Americans died from Japanese bombs and strafing runs at Oahu's Hickam Field. The P-36s and P-40s on the ground had almost no fuel. Their machine guns had been removed for maintenance.

up the runway at Hickam. "You have three Japs on your tail," someone radioed from the control tower. Bullets splatted all around as his B-17 shed altitude on its way to a safe, if hairy, landing. The plane had barely rolled to a stop before he and his crew dashed through the hatch and raced for cover.

Other members of the squadron received similar receptions. Zeroes harassed some of them on their way in. Others came in unmolested, amazed by the realism of the drill the military was staging—someone had even set up smoke pots and mocked up some bombed-out planes on the airfield. News from the tower that "unidentified enemy planes" were attacking dispelled those hopeful guesses as to what was happening.

All twelve B-17s landed safely, although not without some adventures. One crashlanded on a golf course. Another caught fire when Japanese bullets touched off some magnesium flares. The plane skidded down the runway with its tail in flames. It broke in half but came to a safe stop. A Zero peppered flight surgeon William Schick with bullets before he could reach safety.

Adding to the confusion, eighteen scout planes from *Enterprise* showed up over Oahu at around the same time. The big carrier was supposed to have arrived back at Pearl Harbor

ABOVE | Military commanders feared sabotage operations, so they bunched their aircraft. Wheeler Field in Oahu was the first target the Japanese hit on December 7.

around seven thirty that morning but got delayed by heavy seas. Zeroes pounced as the American planes approached Ford Island, blistering their wings with holes. Their fuel tanks were nearly empty, so they had no choice but to press on and hope for the best.

Ensign Manuel Gonzales wasn't supposed to be part of that flight. He had persuaded a friend to give up his spot so he could get home to his wife in Honolulu. In the mayhem of the moment, Gonzales's plane slipped out of everyone's view. Then his voice crackled on the radio. "Don't shoot!" he shouted. "I'm a friendly plane!"

And then he was gone.

It had taken less than half an hour for the Japanese to dish out a terrible thumping. Much of the United States' Pacific Fleet was burning, and much of its air power would never again leave the ground. Oahu's defenders could muster only a sporadic and disorganized defense. They had plenty of fight in them but hadn't done much damage. All they could do was seek cover, keep firing, and wait for the enemy to exhaust itself. But Fuchida and the other Japanese airmen knew something the Americans did not.

The second wave was coming.

ABOVE | American sailors mounted a furious, if improvised, counterattack on the Japanese planes. Here, personnel on Ford Island reload ammunition clips and belts in preparation for the second wave.

CHAPTER 7
THE SECOND WAVE

An unbroken blanket of cloud cover had hampered Commander Mitsuo Fuchida's run toward Oahu. A similar problem faced his close friend Lieutenant Commander Takashige Egusa, who was guiding seventy-eight Aichi D3A dive-bombers as part of a 167-plane second wave of attackers. But rather than white clouds, Egusa was squinting into a haze of inky smoke so thick he could barely discern the remnants of the wounded American fleet sprawled out below him.

Egusa cut a remarkable figure both in and out of combat. His D3A bore a gaudy pattern of red flames that gave it the look of a lightning bolt in an evening storm. He was equally flamboyant on the ground, sporting a wide moustache that would have looked more appropriate in a Buffalo Bill show than in the straitlaced Japanese military. Egusa was daring and brave, kindhearted and charitable. Fuchida often bailed him out with loans because he had given away all his money.

Egusa had been a subpar navy officer until someone decided to put him in a dive-bomber. According to Commander Minoru Genda, Egusa displayed "an almost intuitive grasp of precisely the right thing to do in flight under almost any set of circumstances." Precision dive-bombing came

naturally to him. Egusa honed his skills in the war with China before getting transferred to Operation Hawaii, where he was tasked with upping the accuracy rate of dive-bombers. He proved an outstanding instructor.

The second wave was about halfway to Oahu when Fuchida initiated the initial attack. Holding steady at ten thousand feet, Egusa reviewed his mission as his plane's three-man crew sped south. His main job was finishing what the first wave had started by ripping such gaping holes in damaged battleships and destroyers that they would become unsalvageable.

As Hawaii came into view, he could see that Fuchida had done better than anyone could have expected. Finally spotting a target

through the haze, Egusa tipped his bomber into its dive. Hell was returning to Oahu.

Egusa and every other Japanese airman knew there would be no surprise this time. Bullets began whizzing skyward the moment the second wave came into view. Captain Charles Reordan oversaw the defense of *Tennessee* while wearing an incongruous Panama hat, but the hail of gunfire spewing from the battleship was no joke. Its five-inch guns boomed so frequently that long ribbons of paint were melting off of them. *Pennsylvania*, firing from its position of relative safety in dry dock, was in a

ABOVE | A Japanese Zero, one of forty-one fighter planes that reached its target as part of Japan's aerial force, takes off from the carrier *Akagi* on its way to Oahu.

similar situation, with its guns waving and shimmering from the heat.

Egusa's men focused on the ships that mounted the stiffest opposition, correctly assuming that those were the least damaged. While Zeroes swarmed overhead in case the Americans launched a concerted aerial defense, the D3As unleashed their 250-kilogram bombs on the fleet.

Nevada, the oldest vessel in the battleship fleet, drew the most attention. She was the farthest north in Battleship Row, anchored just ahead of the devastated *Arizona*. A thrill

coursed around the base when, at 8:50 a.m., with the second wave blazing all around it, the twenty-seven-year-old veteran of World War I began steaming toward the exit of the harbor. On its face this was an impossible achievement. It usually took hours for a battleship to get up steam. But the vessel's firemen already had two boilers hot when the first wave arrived. One boiler always stayed lit so the ship had power while in port. The other was going because of Ensign Joseph Taussig, who had fired a second boiler in anticipation of switching power to it later in the morning.

ABOVE | A bomb exploded belowdecks of the battleship *Nevada*. The force of the blast ripped through the forecastle deck. *Nevada*'s dash for the harbor's exit provided a brief but memorable moment of inspiration amid the chaos.

Whether from efficiency or good luck, Taussig's order gave *Nevada*'s crew the head start needed to get the ship underway. It chugged off amid a hail of gunfire without its captain and executive officer, who were still on shore.

Chief Boatswain Edwin J. Hill recognized that *Nevada* needed every officer it could get. As the ship began groaning away from its anchorage, he noticed from the deck that there was no one at the wharf to slip the tether. Hill gathered a few men, clambered onto the dock, and unmoored the vessel. As *Nevada* picked up momentum, Hill dove into the water and began swimming after it. Remarkably, he caught up, was hauled aboard, and resumed his duties.

Nevada had already provided one iconic Pearl Harbor moment. Its band had been playing the national anthem when the very first torpedoes splashed into the water that morning. The musicians paused for a moment before resuming with barely a hitch. Everyone held formation until the last note. Indeed, the ship was the "home of the brave."

Now the aged battleship provided a second indelible memory. With its tattered flag flapping in the breeze—for its flag was

ABOVE | Seven brothers from rural Iowa—Allen, Ray, Bick, Ted, Gilbert, Bruce, and Marvin Patten—aboard *Nevada* a few weeks before the attack. Ted's hitch ended before December 7. He reenlisted on December 8. An eighth brother joined in 1942. All of them survived the war.

still there—*Nevada* limped toward the open ocean. Ensign Taussig lay at his battle station, his left leg mutilated by a bullet wound. Turning to a friend, he deadpanned, "Isn't this a hell of a thing—the man in charge lying flat on his back while everyone else is doing something."

As the only battleship moving, *Nevada* drew heavy fire. Its crew's audacious maneuver could have backfired if the Japanese had been able to sink it and bottle up the harbor at least partway. It was already sailing with an enormous hole in its bow. Crews had

counterflooded the ship to keep it upright, if low in the water. Now bombs began falling all over it. One of them killed Edwin Hill and forty-six other crewmen. Fires around the deck pumped acrid smoke poured into the sky.

Nevada limped past *Arizona* with guns blazing. Men waved and cheered from the hull of *Oklahoma*. The fires onboard *Nevada* grew so intense that gunners threw themselves atop their shells to prevent them from exploding from the heat. Despite such heroics, it soon became clear that escape

ABOVE | Rescuers atop the capsized *Oklahoma*. Inside, the scene was horrifying, as trapped sailors conserved precious oxygen and searched for any way out of the watery tomb.

was impossible. Signal flags hoisted atop the Naval District water tower ordered the ship out of the channel. At 9:10 a.m., a pilot grounded *Nevada* in the shallows off Hospital Point, just southwest of Ford Island and near the entrance to the channel. With its run for freedom prematurely ended, the ship slowly settled into the mud.

Much of Oahu, including the city of Honolulu, remained curiously calm. Many residents interpreted the action as an especially noisy training session. Local radio stations were providing some information but little concrete news. The first report of serious trouble came at 8:40 a.m., just as Takashige Egusa was sending the second wave into action. This broadcast created as much confusion as it did enlightenment. "A sporadic air attack has been made on Oahu," intoned a KGU announcer. "Enemy airplanes have been shot down . . . the rising sun has been sighted on the wingtips." Some listeners thought that "sporadic" meant "simulated," thereby giving credence to the conviction that all the noise was coming from some kind of drill.

Shocking as it is to us, with our twenty-four-hour news cycle and never-ending crawl of top stories across the screen, Honolulu's KGU and KGMB cycled between music, nebulous updates on the "sporadic air

ABOVE | American antiaircraft fire brought down this Japanese Type 99 Carrier Bomber (top) and Type 97 Carrier Attack Plane (bottom left), both launched from the carrier *Kaga*, along with this Zero (bottom right), launched from the carrier *Akagi*.

attack," and Sunday prayer services. A casual listener could have missed the news entirely, at least for a while. Japanese officers listening on the carrier *Akagi* found the lack of panic puzzling, and a little disconcerting.

Commander Mitsuo Fuchida knew better. His crew kept circling after the rest of the first wave disengaged. The plane was in rough shape—a control cable had been shot away—but Fuchida was determined to stick out the rest of the attack. As the second wave began its withdrawal, he ordered one last pass over Oahu so he could photograph the damage below. No American planes were in the sky, so he knew his men had established air superiority. Although flames engulfed the airfields scattered around the island, Fuchida could see that many of the hangars remained untouched. He counted *Arizona*, *Nevada*, *Oklahoma*, and *West Virginia* as sunk, and considered *California*, *Maryland*, *Pennsylvania*, and *Tennessee* so badly damaged that they would require serious repairs before they would sail again. Many cruisers and destroyers had been hit, but exactly which ships, and how badly, he could not say. He assumed that some of Japan's midget submarines were inside the harbor waiting to inflict more damage.

As Fuchida winged toward the rendezvous point to gather a few stragglers before heading north, he was already compiling a

ABOVE AND RIGHT | The battleship *Nevada* steams through bombs and wreckage in this charcoal-and-chalk drawing by Commander Griffith Bailey Coale. In the foreground is *Oglala*, flagship of the Pacific Fleet Mine Force, downed by a torpedo and a bomb burst. Salvage crews spent thousands of man-hours raising *Oglala*, which returned to service and operated in the Pacific Theater for the rest of the war.

mental checklist of potential targets for the next assault. There were the aircraft carriers, of course, but no one could say where *Enterprise* and *Lexington* were right now. Of more immediate concern were the harbor's repair shops, refueling facilities, and dockyards. Taking them out would force the Americans all the way back to California, leaving the Pacific as a Japanese lake.

Few of the Americans on the ground were thinking in such grandiose terms. All around the island, pressing crises demanded immediate attention. Fires raged onboard ships and in the water. Pools of blazing fuel imperiled everything still afloat. Survivors trapped inside overturned vessels tapped at the hulls,

desperately signaling rescuers. Wounded men bobbed in the harbor and lay prostrate on runways. Doctors soothed burn victims and attended mangled limbs. While dousing these literal and figurative fires, the Americans did their best to suppress the disturbing thought that a third wave was a near certainty.

Fuchida's plane rolled across *Akagi*'s deck at around noon. Crews were refueling and rearming planes in preparation for another takeoff. Fuchida escaped the knot of admirers that surrounded him so he could compose his battle report in the relative calm of

the launch command center. He had barely begun when he got the request: "Come to the bridge quickly."

Admiral Nagumo was waiting for him there. "How did the battle go?" he asked. Fuchida briefly described the extensive damage inflicted on the enemy's air and sea forces. Nagumo nodded in appreciation while the airman spoke. "Commander, well done," he said.

What next? Fuchida pushed for an aggressive approach. "All things considered we have achieved a great amount of destruction, but it would be unwise to assume that we have destroyed everything," he explained. "There are still many targets remaining which should be hit. Therefore I recommend that another attack be launched."

Nagumo wasn't so sure. "Do you think that the US Fleet could not come out from Pearl Harbor within six months?" he asked. That had been the goal all along, clearing the way for Japan's conquest of Southeast Asia and the South Pacific. Fuchida sensed the momentum for a third wave slipping away but gave an honest response. "The main force of the US Pacific Fleet will not be able to come out within six months," he agreed.

That was exactly what Nagumo wanted to hear. He had already hurt the Americans worse than anyone had expected, and at a much lower cost than he had feared. Only twenty-nine of the 344 planes that had launched from his decks had failed to return. With the element of surprise lost, renewing the offensive would surely up the toll. Moreover, refitting the planes for another run would delay takeoff until after sunset, making the mission that much more dangerous. The weather was deteriorating. And a counteroffensive from *Enterprise* and *Lexington* could hit at any moment. Hunt down the American carriers, some of his subordinates urged. No, Nagumo insisted, it is time for the task force to leave. He ordered signal flags raised that would redirect the fleet toward home.

"I was totally against this judgment," Fuchida later wrote. But orders were orders. The Americans braced for a blow that never came. Admiral Chester Nimitz later said in an interview with historian Gordon Prange that "the fact that the Japanese did not return to Pearl Harbor and complete the job was the greatest help to us, for they left their

principal enemy with the time to catch his breath, restore his morale, and rebuild his forces."

Nagumo suspected the enemy was looking for him. They were, in a way, but without success. At the moment the admiral made his fateful decision, the most concerted American reconnaissance mission in the sky consisted of a single pilot, Marine Sergeant Thomas Hailey. When Hailey's ship, *Oklahoma*, capsized, he dove into the water and swam for *Maryland*, which was docked just inside the dying battleship, between *Oklahoma* and the shore. After rescuing some of his crewmates, he manned an antiaircraft gun of a type he had never before used and began hammering away at Zeroes.

ABOVE | Japanese pilots celebrated their triumph at Pearl Harbor. They had trained for months and were proud to serve their emperor. Many became national heroes.

Once the Japanese flew away, Hailey picked his way through flames and rubble until he reached the naval air station. Still carrying a rifle, he volunteered to take up a plane and pursue the enemy fleet. By 11:30 a.m. he was in a Sikorsky with the open ocean unfurling beneath him. For five hours he searched before returning empty-handed to Ford Island, still clad only in the oil-soaked underwear he had been wearing since before the first torpedo struck *Oklahoma*.

Tadao Fuchikami, the delivery boy bearing the coded message from General Marshall, had spent the day fighting through traffic jams, roadblocks, and accusations that he was a Japanese paratrooper. Fifteen minutes after Sergeant Hailey took off, he finally maneuvered his Indian Scout motorcycle through the entrance gates of Fort Shafter. He putt-putted to the message center, handed over the cable, and headed back to the office.

Decoding the message took an additional three hours. It was nearly 3:00 p.m. before Lieutenant General Short received a decrypted copy. Short summoned a courier who ran it to Admiral Kimmel's office. Painters were blacking out the admiral's windows, a necessary precaution now that war had

come. Kimmel scanned Marshall's words: "Just what significance the hour set may have we do not know, but be on the alert accordingly." By now the significance was clear, and the general's warning pointless. Kimmel hurled the message in the trash can. "I surely was entitled to know of the hour fixed by Japan for the probable outbreak of war against the United States," he grumbled in his memoirs.

Oahu's radio stations had gone off the air, a sensible precaution that discouraged would-be attackers from homing in on their signal. Radio silence also created a vacuum in which rumors proliferated. Honolulu, having shaken off its initial disbelief, was in a full-fledged panic. There had been explosions around the city. No one could blame residents for not knowing that nearly all of those explosions resulted from poorly aimed American artillery. Reports of a Japanese land assault circulated. Local Japanese were rising up. Spies had poisoned the drinking water. Sabotage rings were scheming. Disloyal Japanese had cut arrows into sugarcane fields, or ringed the island with small boats, or in some other way pointed the Zeroes and bombers in the correct direction, as if the Japanese

military was incapable of finding Pearl Harbor and the airfields on its own.

None of these stories were true, but with everyone scanning the sky for the next attack, it is easy to understand why paranoia was so prevalent. No one had thought the Japanese capable of such a well-planned, brutally effective strike. They must have had inside help, the thinking went. Island authorities began rounding up people of Japanese descent, particularly journalists, language teachers, and Shinto priests. Several hundred would be taken into custody over the next few days. None were ever connected to any foreign plot.

Seaman George Murphy, twenty-one years old and just beginning to fill out his six-foot-two-inch frame, looked every bit the warrior. In reality, he hoped his job as a printer aboard *Oklahoma* would propel him toward his dream of working for a newspaper. Murphy was in the ship's print shop when "air attack! air attack!" came blaring through the loudspeakers. He began making his way topside only to find the ladders jammed with sailors. As he retreated below, a sudden wave of shocks rocked the ship, leaving him disoriented.

ABOVE | Crews struggled to free survivors from the capsized *Oklahoma*. Moored next to it, *Maryland* also suffered serious damage but took few casualties. Its crew fired the ship's antiaircraft batteries throughout the attack.

Murphy found himself neck deep in water with about thirty other people, all of them drawing life from a small air bubble below the tile ceiling. A handful of corpses bobbed around the room. One seaman swung a flashlight around the space, which looked unfamiliar.

After an hour of waiting for rescue, the imprisoned sailors began thinking of escape. Someone located a porthole beneath the waterline. No one wanted to be the first man through. The air was growing foul. It occurred to someone that the porthole was hung the wrong way, which could only mean that *Oklahoma* was upside down—the tile ceiling was actually the floor of the dispensary.

One after another they squeezed through the fourteen-inch circle. Some people were simply too large to fit. It took Murphy three tries before he finally popped out the other side. Swimming to the surface, he was amazed to discover how extensive the destruction was; he had assumed *Oklahoma* was the only ship that suffered damage. A launch scooped him up. He survived the war, then spent decades at the *Manteca Bulletin* in California.

Several hundred of his crewmates remained inside the ship. They tapped on the hull with wrenches and anything else they could find. On the other side, men were tapping back, offering encouragement, and marking survivors' locations as best they could.

Salvage teams swarmed over *Oklahoma*'s hull. Rescue proved fiendishly difficult. At first crews employed acetylene torches, the fastest means of reaching the men, but the tools sucked oxygen out of airspaces and asphyxiated the victims. Slower tools such as jackhammers allowed air to rush out of the holes they made, causing the water level inside to rise and drowning some sailors.

Crews worked without respite while the trapped men endured a hellish night. They investigated every possible way out; they sat as still as they could; they buried themselves in their thoughts; and they prayed for deliverance. Rescuers pulled thirty-two survivors from the wreckage over the next few days. For several hundred others, there would be no escape.

Fires still burned on *Arizona* and other ships as night fell on Oahu. The chaos of that morning had morphed into a confused mixture of resolution, anger, and fear. Emergency crews were still hard at work across the island, determined to save every soul

they could. Cries for revenge were heard all around what had so recently been a Pacific paradise. Admiral Bull Halsey articulated this desire as well as anyone. "Before we're through with 'em, the Japanese language will be spoken only in hell!" he roared.

The rumors grew more expansive as the darkness deepened. So-called reliable sources reported that the Panama Canal had been bombed. Or maybe it was San Francisco. Gunfire bursts shattered the quiet as over-zealous guards fired on deer, mongooses, and other animals that sounded too much

like invaders for their comfort. A patrol plane blew up a fishing boat, killing four. A machine gunner on *California* mowed down two survivors from *Utah*. Antiaircraft crews shot down four planes returning to Oahu from the carrier *Enterprise*.

Admiral Nagumo's fleet was five hundred miles away by then, plowing west and hoping to avoid additional contact with the enemy. His planes had sunk four battleships, three

---

ABOVE | Crowds in New York City's Times Square grab copies of the *New York Enquirer*. Initial news reports were scattered and contradictory. Americans on both coasts feared follow-up attacks.

destroyers, and three cruisers and destroyed nearly two hundred airplanes.

Over the coming months and years the United States Navy replaced the lost planes and returned all the damaged battleships to service except *Arizona*, *Oklahoma*, and *Utah*; the latter had already been a target ship rather than an active combat vessel. But no repair crew could restore 2,403 lost American lives. Nearly half of those were on *Arizona*, with 429 more coming from *Oklahoma*'s ranks.

Nagumo's men left behind an island in ruins and a nation changed. The war so many Americans dreaded had reached their shores. They would fight back—of that they were sure. Rather than destroy their morale, as the Japanese had hoped, Pearl Harbor had given them a new sense of unity and purpose. Now Americans' eyes turned toward Washington, where the man who had already steered the United States through the worst economic disaster in history would soon send the country into the most destructive war the world had ever seen.

ABOVE | The attack killed 2,403 Americans and drew the nation into World War II. "Remember Pearl Harbor!" became both a rallying cry and a somber admonition to honor those who lost their lives.

Honolulu Star-Bulletin, Wednesday, Aug. 15, 1945—11

Honolulu Star-Bulletin 1st EXTRA

8 PAGES—HONOLULU, TERRITORY OF HAWAII, U. S. A., SUNDAY, DECEMBER 7, 1941—8 PAGES ★ PRICE FIVE CENTS

WAR!

OAHU BOMBED BY JAPANESE PLANES

(Associated Press by Transpacific Telephone)

SAN FRANCISCO, Dec. 7.—President Roosevelt announced this morning that Japanese planes had attacked Manila and Pearl Harbor.

SIX KNOWN DEAD, 21 INJURED, AT EMERGENCY HOSPITAL

Attack Made On Island's Defense Areas

By UNITED PRESS

WASHINGTON, Dec. 7.—Text of a White House announcement detailing the attack on the Hawaiian islands is:

"The Japanese attacked Pearl Harbor from the air and all naval and military activities on the island of Oahu, principal American base in the Hawaiian islands."

Oahu was attacked at 7:55 this morning by Japanese planes.

The Rising Sun, emblem of Japan, was seen on plane wing tips.

Wave after wave of bombers streamed through the clouded morning sky from the southwest and flung their missiles on a city resting in peaceful Sabbath calm.

According to an unconfirmed report received at the governor's office, the Japanese force that attacked Oahu reached island waters aboard two small airplane carriers.

It was also reported that at the governor's office either an attempt had been made to bomb the USS Lexington, or that it had been bombed.

CITY IN UPROAR

Within 10 minutes the city was in an uproar. As bombs fell in many parts of the city, and in defense areas the defenders of the islands went into quick action.

Army intelligence officers at Ft. Shafter announced officially shortly after 9 a. m. the fact of the bombardment by an enemy but long previous army and navy had taken immediate measures in defense.

"Oahu is under a sporadic air raid," the announcement said.

"Civilians are ordered to stay off the streets until further notice."

CIVILIANS ORDERED OFF STREETS

The army has ordered that all civilians stay off the streets and highways and not use telephones.

Evidence that the Japanese attack has registered some hits was shown by three billowing pillars of smoke in the Pearl Harbor and Hickam field area.

All navy personnel and civilian defense workers, with the exception of women, have been ordered to duty at Pearl Harbor.

The Pearl Harbor highway was immediately a mass of racing cars.

A trickling stream of injured people began pouring into the city emergency hospital a few minutes after the bombardment started.

Thousands of telephone calls almost swamped the Mutual Telephone Co., which put extra operators on duty.

At The Star-Bulletin office the phone calls deluged the single operator and it was impossible for this newspaper, for sometime, to handle the flood of calls. Here also an emergency operator was called.

HOUR OF ATTACK—7:55 A. M.

An official army report from department headquarters, made public shortly before 11, is that the first attack was at 7:55 a. m.

Witnesses said they saw at least 50 airplanes over Pearl Harbor.

The attack centered in the Pearl Harbor, Army authorities said:

"The rising sun was seen on the wing tips of the airplanes."

Although martial law has not been declared officially, the city of Honolulu was operating under M-Day conditions.

It is reliably reported that enemy objectives under attack were Wheeler field Hickam field, Kaneohe bay and naval air station and Pearl Harbor.

Some enemy planes were reported shot down.

The body of the pilot was seen in a plane burning at Wahiawa.

Oahu appeared to be taking calmly after the first uproar of queries.

ANTIAIRCRAFT GUNS IN ACTION

First indication of the raid came shortly before 8 this morning when antiaircraft guns around Pearl Habor began sending up a thunderous barrage.

At the same time a vast cloud of black smoke arose from the naval base and also from Hickam field where flames could be seen.

BOMB NEAR GOVERNOR'S MANSION

Shortly before 9:30 a bomb fell near Washington Place, the residence of the governor. Governor Poindexter and Secretary Charles M. Hite were there.

It was reported that the bomb killed an unidentified Chinese man across the street in front of the Schuman Carriage Co. where windows were broken.

C. E. Daniels, a welder, found a fragment of shell or bomb at South and Queen Sts. which he brought into the City Hall. This fragrent weighed about a pound.

At 10:05 a. m. today Governor Poindexter telephoned to The Star-Bulletin announcing he has declared a state of emergency for the entire territory.

He announced that Edouard L. Doty, executive secretary of the major disaster council, has been appointed director under the M-Day law's provisions.

Governor Poindexter urged all residents of Honolulu to remain off the street, and the people of the territory to remain calm.

Mr. Doty reported that all major disaster council wardens and medical units were on duty within a half hour of the time the alarm was given.

Workers employed at Pearl Harbor were ordered at 10:10 a. m. not to report at Pearl Harbor.

The mayor's major disaster council was to meet at the city hall at about 10:30 this morning.

At least two Japanese planes were reported at Hawaiian department headquarters to have been shot down.

One of the planes was shot down at Ft. Kamehameha and the other back of the Wai—

Hundreds See City Bombed

Hundreds of Honolulans who hurried to the top of Punchbowl soon after bombs began to fall, saw spread out before them the whole panorama of surprise attack and defense.

Far off over Pearl Harbor the white sky was polka-dotted with anti-aircraft smoke.

Rolling away from the navy base were billowing clouds of oily black smoke. Sometimes a burst of flame reddened the black scarves of the smoke.

Out from the silver-ribbed mouth of the harbor a flotilla of destroyers streamed in haste, smoke pouring from their stacks...

Names of Dead and Injured

The city emergency hospital reported at 10:30 a list of 6 killed and 21 injured.

The casualties that will be carried later. Here is a partial list:

Peter Lopes, 24, of 3461 Kamanea Rd St., was reported at 9:30 A. M. to be in serious condition from wounds in the upper abdomen.

Bernice Gouveia, 22, 1762 Mahaku St., is suffering from a fractured thigh, lacerations on the right leg and left arm.

A Portuguese girl, unidentified, 18 years old, died on arrival from puncture wounds.

Another victim who died on arrival was Frank Ohashi, 30, 2766 Kamanuki St., from punctures wounds in the chest.

Cecilia Broadby, 30, Moanalua Gardens, was released from the hospital after treatment for lacerations.

Three were reported injured and reported killed from the bomb that fell at Fort and School Sts.

Schools Closed

All schools on Oahu, both public and private, will remain closed until further notice, Edward L. Doty, territorial director of civilian defense, announced at 11 a. m. today. This does not apply elsewhere in the territory.

Editorial

HAWAII MEETS THE CRISIS

Honolulu and Hawaii will meet the emergency of war today as Honolulu and Hawaii have met emergencies in the past—coolly, calmly and with immediate and complete support of the officials, officers and troops who are in charge.

Governor Poindexter and the army and navy leaders have called upon the public to remain calm, for civilians who have no essential business on the streets to stay off; and for every man and woman to do his duty.

That request, coupled with the measures promptly taken to meet the situation that has suddenly and terribly developed, will be needed.

Hawaii will do its part—as a loyal American territory.

In this crisis, every difference of race, creed and color will be submerged in the one desire and determination to play the part that Americans always play in crisis.

BULLETIN

Additional Star-Bulletin extras today will cover the latest developments in this war move.

This page reproduced with our compliments as a V-Day souvenir

R. A. HOWE & CO. Hawaii
WHOLESALERS AND DISTRIBUTORS

ABOVE | A people who had hoped to stay out of the war now had no choice but to focus on it. As the strip at the bottom of this V-Day reprint suggests, however, Pearl Harbor was also the beginning of the end for Japanese militarism.

CHAPTER 8
A DATE WHICH WILL LIVE IN INFAMY

On the evening of December 6, 1941, after hosting a dinner for thirty-two guests, President Roosevelt retired to his study to relax. He was bone weary, worn out by the worsening crises with Germany in the Atlantic and Japan in the Pacific. Resting in his study, he flipped through his stamp collection and talked with Harry Hopkins, his most trusted aide. They were a grim couple—FDR crippled by polio and showing the wear of ten years in office, and Hopkins withered by a struggle with stomach cancer but still chain-smoking Lucky Strike cigarettes.

At 9:30 p.m. there was a knock on the door. Lieutenant Lester Schulz delivered a recently arrived top-secret communiqué to the president. It was the first thirteen telegrams of a fourteen-telegram message from Tokyo to the Japanese Embassy in Washington. Slowly FDR read the document, which concluded that "because of American attitudes" there was no hope of achieving a diplomatic solution to the pressing problems between Japan and the United States.

LEFT | Monday morning, December 8, 1941. One headline reads, "ENEMY PLANES NEAR N.Y. FROM ATLANTIC." The other focuses on the Pacific.

The crucial fourteenth telegram of the message was missing, but its overall intent was clear to Roosevelt. Finishing the final page, he handed it to Hopkins, watching as his confidant's eyes raced across the pages. When he finished he passed it back to the president. Their eyes met. "This means war," FDR said.

War, certainly, but where, and when? At that moment the security of Pearl Harbor was far from the front of Roosevelt's mind. *If* the Japanese attacked anywhere—and that was a very large if—FDR thought they would most likely pick the easiest target close to their home islands. Holland and France were either wholly or partially controlled by the Nazis, and Great Britain, while standing firm, was battling for its life. None of the European imperial powers were in any position to defend their Asian colonial territories. As far as the Japanese were concerned, British Malaya, Singapore, and Hong Kong, French Indochina, and the Dutch East Indies were low-hanging fruit, ripe for the plucking.

What made the thought of those targets even more agonizing to Roosevelt was that he

ABOVE | His face sober, President Franklin D. Roosevelt signs the declaration of war against Japan. He would not live to see the end of the conflict.

knew if the Japanese struck those European outposts, there was nothing he could do to stop them. He realized that Japanese assaults toward the oil fields of the Dutch East Indies, the rubber plantations of British Malaya, or the tin mines of Indochina would ultimately threaten America's economic position in the Western Pacific. But what could he do? It was hard enough for him to rally tepid congressional support to aid Great Britain. And opinion polls made it clear that most US citizens did not want to risk American lives fighting Germany on the Atlantic or in Europe. "Why, then," FDR's speechwriter Robert Sherwood observed, "should Americans die for Thailand, or for such outposts of British imperialism as Singapore or Hong Kong or of Dutch imperialism in the East Indies, or for Communism in Vladivostok?"

As the president prepared for sleep late at night on December 6, undoubtedly Japan's intentions troubled him. But he was not worried about the short-term fate of the United States. America was at peace and, regardless of Roosevelt's plans or desires, almost certain to remain so for the foreseeable future.

Those were his thoughts, and they were shared by virtually all of the nation's military planners. When Secretary of the Navy Frank Knox consulted with his team, he had only one overriding question: "Gentlemen, are

they going to hit us?" His advisors were in complete agreement that Japan would not attack the United States. "No, Mr. Secretary," said his head of war planning. "They are going to attack the British. They are not ready for us yet."

Roosevelt's official schedule for Sunday, December 7, was appropriately light. He awoke to a bright day, sunshine warming his bedroom. The country was at peace, the economy was humming along, and the president seemed to have the nation's affairs under control. He had a 12:30 p.m. appointment with the Chinese ambassador, Dr. Hu Shih, but no other significant engagements. He had given most of his aides, including his speechwriters, the day off, and the

ABOVE | Secretary of the Navy Franklin "Frank" Knox. On the night of December 6, his advisors predicted that Japan would not attack the United States.

White House press had followed suit. Since they expected nothing to report, they stayed home, planning to enjoy an uneventful day.

FDR met with the Chinese ambassador in the second-floor oval study, adjacent to the president's bedroom. It was his favorite room, a private nook overflowing with books, stamp albums, stacks of papers, and ship models. Nautical prints hanging from hooks gave the small room the feel of an admiral's quarters; leather sofas and chairs, acquired from Theodore Roosevelt's presidential yacht, lent an air of a men's clubroom to the place. It was comfortable, fitting an informal man. The oval study, speechwriter Robert Sherwood wrote, was "the focal point of the nation and, in a sense, of the whole world."

Dressed casually in a pair of flannel slacks and an old gray pullover sweater, FDR discussed Asian affairs with Dr. Shih. He admitted that diplomatic negotiations with Japan were going nowhere, and although he had sent a personal appeal to Emperor Hirohito, he doubted it would reverse America's deteriorating relations with Japan. "This is my last effort at peace," he told Dr. Shih. "I am afraid it will fail." War, the president thought, was inevitable. "I think that something nasty will develop in Burma, or the Dutch East Indies, or possibly even in the Philippines."

Something someplace—it was still vague and abstract when the ambassador departed the White House at 1:10 p.m. Freed from official business, FDR retired to the oval study with Hopkins, talking, his advisor wrote, "about things far removed from war." After eating he toyed with his stamps, and Hopkins reclined in a sofa and smoked a cigarette. Both men believed that Japan was preparing to strike somewhere in the Pacific. But neither thought it would attack an American outpost.

While Roosevelt examined stamps, Secretary Knox received an urgent message from Pearl Harbor via the Naval Station in San Francisco. An aide recalled that the dispatch went "something like 'We are being attacked. This is no drill.'"

"My God," Knox exclaimed, "this can't be true, this must mean the Philippines." But the message had carried the CinCPAC—Commander in Chief, US Pacific Fleet—origin designate. Admiral Harold R. Stark, Chief of Naval Operations, knew the message did not originate in the Philippines. Firmly he corrected Knox, "No, sir; this is Pearl."

At 1:47 p.m., less than a half hour after the first Japanese bombs exploded on Pearl Harbor, Secretary Knox called the White House, and an operator immediately

connected him with Roosevelt. The secretary had news from the San Francisco Naval Station. "Mr. President," Knox said, "they had picked up a radio [report] from Honolulu from the Commander in Chief of our forces there advising all our stations that an air attack was on and that it was 'no drill.'" It seemed "as if the Japanese have attacked Pearl Harbor."

"NO!" Roosevelt shouted.

Once off the phone, however, Roosevelt regained his composure, assuming the "deadly calm" his wife had always noticed in times of trial. It was as if his mind worked best, his analytical skills became the sharpest, when he confronted a crisis. Hopkins retreated into denial, saying that the message must be a mistake and the Japanese could not have attacked Pearl Harbor. FDR disagreed. "The President thought the report was probably true," Hopkins wrote, "and thought it was just the kind of unexpected thing the Japanese would do, and at the very time they were discussing peace in the Pacific they were plotting to overthrow it."

No sooner was Roosevelt off the phone

ABOVE | Roosevelt loved his stamp collection. Even during moments of crisis, looking through his stamps brought him an inner calm.

problems translating and retyping the final fourteenth telegram had forced them to delay the meeting. By the time they arrived in the reception room to Hull's office it was 2:20 p.m., almost an hour after Japan had attacked Pearl Harbor.

Not only had the Japanese bungled the delivery of the message and reached the State Department after the bombing had commenced, they also arrived after Roosevelt had told Hull of the surprise attack. Hull was unsure how to proceed. Nothing about the meeting had diplomatic precedent. The idea of delivering a virtual war message while bombs were in the air and men dying on land and sea smacked of the Kafkaesque.

Roosevelt calmly told Hull to meet with the diplomats but not to mention Pearl Harbor. He was simply "to receive their reply formally and coolly and bow them out." FDR's instructions were coldly diplomatic, but Hull was burning with outrage.

When Nomura and Kurusu entered Hull's office, the secretary received them with an icy greeting, forcing them to conduct their business on their feet and not offering them chairs. Apologizing for the delay, Nomura handed Hull the final message, explaining that he had planned on delivering it at 1:00 p.m. Why specifically 1:00 p.m.? Hull asked. Nomura said he didn't know; those were

with Knox than he called Secretary of War Henry Stimson, then Secretary of State Cordell Hull. "Have you heard the news?" he asked. "They have attacked Hawaii. They are now bombing Hawaii." The news came as a "relief" to Stimson. War with Japan, he thought, was inevitable, perhaps had been inevitable for decades. The "indecision was over." With a united American people behind the administration, the time for action had arrived.

Hull got the news as he was about to meet with Japanese Ambassador Kichisaburo Nomura and special "peace" envoy Saburo Kurusu. They had a message to deliver, one that was supposed to have been delivered at 1:00 p.m. (7:30 a.m. Hawaiian time, or twenty-five minutes before the attack). But

ABOVE | A member of the foreign policy establishment, Secretary of War Henry Stimson had served under presidents William Howard Taft and Herbert Hoover before joining the Roosevelt cabinet.

simply the instructions he had received from Tokyo. Hull brushed the answer aside, drilling home the point that it was now after 2:00 p.m. But he accepted the message and made a show of examining it.

Then he spoke his mind: "In all my fifty years of public service I have never seen a document that was more crowded with infamous falsehoods and distortions—infamous falsehoods and distortions on a scale so huge that I never imagined until today that any Government on this planet was capable of uttering them."

Nomura began to protest but Hull cut him off with the wave of a hand. Then he nodded toward the door. Heads down, the Japanese diplomats departed the room. Nomura, especially, was clearly "under great emotional strain." Only after he left the State Department and returned home did he learn of the attack on Pearl Harbor. "[T]his might have reached Hull's ears during our conversation," he later wrote in his diary.

Back in the White House Roosevelt gathered his war team, scouring America's far-flung bases for information and planning his next move. Reports from Pearl, sketchy as they were, indicated that the Japanese had pounded the American base, but they were frustratingly vague on details. How had they evaded American security?

Was the strike a prelude to a land invasion? Was California next? If not, where exactly did Japan plan to move next? Two facts were glaringly clear: The assault on Pearl Harbor was an act of war, and no nation mounts an offensive war without a clearly outlined plan. Pearl Harbor was the beginning, not the end, of Japan's offensive.

Army Chief of Staff General George Marshall, as thin as he was formal, arrived at the White House shortly before 3:00 p.m. and confirmed the few facts that FDR had learned. The Japanese bombers had attacked shortly before 8:00 a.m. Hawaiian time, and the attack was still underway. American air and naval bases had suffered considerable damage. Each drip in the slow flow of

ABOVE | Secretary of State Cordell Hull. Japanese diplomats informed him of impending hostilities after the bombs had begun to rain on Pearl Harbor.

information shocked the president, adding new horrors to the disaster. Even the weather seemed to reflect the mood inside the White House. The morning sunshine was gone, replaced by heavy dark clouds and falling temperatures.

Although FDR and his war council fumbled for answers to the most basic questions, they took solace in the fact that the Japanese actions had ended the long debate over America's position in world affairs. There would be no more fence-sitting; the country was headed toward the thick of war. As Hopkins wrote, "The conference met in not too tense an atmosphere because I think that all of us believed that in the last analysis the enemy was Hitler and that he could never be defeated without force of arms; that sooner or later we were bound to be in the war and that Japan had given us an opportunity."

Still, the group had abundant worries. The fate of the Philippines agitated General Marshall. What was happening at the key American position closest to Japan? The war department had not been able to get through to General Douglas MacArthur, head of US forces in the Philippines, and soon rumors of disaster were ricocheting like bullets. And there was the matter of President Roosevelt's war message to the American people, which he would deliver the next day. What exactly should he say? The president preferred something brief, enough to register his anger and unify the people but not something that would dwell on details and become anchored to a sea of facts and plans.

Secretary of State Hull disagreed. Before becoming secretary in 1933, Hull had been a lawyer and congressman, famous for authoring the federal income tax laws of 1913 and 1916 and the inheritance tax of 1916. He was a careful man, apt to be overly legalistic. He argued that FDR should give a long, detailed address, ranging widely over the history of Japanese-US relations and specifically over Japan's intransigence, lack of good faith, and duplicity. Although FDR's mind was made up, others lobbied for Hull's approach.

ABOVE | Chief of Staff of the United States Army George Catlett Marshall was Roosevelt's chief advisor on military affairs, one of the few men that the president could not do without.

After the meeting, as darkness began to gather outside the White House, Roosevelt turned to his speech. His speechwriters were away from town, so he was forced to craft the most important address of his presidency on his own, a prospect that did not disturb him a whit. A gifted speechwriter, he had a wonderful sense of the language and a pitch-perfect feel for his audience. Summoning his secretary Grace Tully into the oval study, he took a long drag from a cigarette and then said, "Sit down, Grace, I'm going before Congress tomorrow. I'd like to dictate my message. It will be short."

His voice was calm, his attitude resolute, his mind focused. Tully later noted that her boss "spoke each word incisively and slowly,

carefully specifying each punctuation mark and paragraph." Seeming to look inwardly as he dictated, he began: "Yesterday comma December seventh comma 1941 dash a date which will live in world history dash the United States of America was simultaneously and deliberately attacked by naval and air forces of the Empire of Japan." He continued his dictation, Tully observed, "without hesitation, interruption or second thoughts." Shortly after beginning he finished with the inevitable sentence, "I ask that the Congress declare that since the unprovoked and dastardly attack by Japan on Sunday comma December seventh comma a state of war has existed between the United States and the Japanese Empire."

ABOVE | FDR's personal secretary Grace Tully took dictation while the president composed the war message he planned to deliver to Congress. He spoke without hesitation or second thoughts.

139

He was tired when he finished, conscious of the burden he shouldered. But when Tully returned with a typed draft of the speech, he selected a pencil and began to edit the manuscript, searching for better ways to make his point. In the first sentence he crossed out "world history" and added in its place "infamy." That was better. More poetic, more memorable. He drew a line through "simultaneously" and replaced it with "suddenly." The first sentence now read: "Yesterday, December seventh, 1941—a date which will live in infamy—the United States of America was suddenly and deliberately attacked by naval and air forces of the Empire of Japan."

He continued to revise, and after dinner he returned for another bout of edits. He added the sentence toward the end: "No matter how long it may take us to overcome this premeditated invasion, the American people will in their righteous might win through to absolute victory." Hopkins also added an inspirational line near the conclusion: "With confidence in our armed forces—with the unbounded determination of our people—we will gain inevitable triumph—so help us

ABOVE | President Roosevelt with his closest political advisor, Harry Hopkins. Although Hopkins was still weak from an operation for stomach cancer, he stayed near to FDR most of December 7. **RIGHT AND FOLLOWING PAGES** | The draft of FDR's "PROPOSED MESSAGE TO THE CONGRESS" with his edits. He added several of the most famous passages in the editing phase. It's hard to imagine the address without the word "infamy."

DRAFT No. 1   December 7, 1941.

PROPOSED MESSAGE TO THE CONGRESS

Yesterday, December 7, 1941, a date which will live in ~~world history~~ *infamy*

the United States of America was ~~simultaneously~~ *suddenly* and deliberately attacked

by naval and air forces of the Empire of Japan ~~without warning~~

The United States was at the moment at peace with that nation and was

~~continuing the~~ *still in* conversations with its Government and its Emperor looking

toward the maintenance of peace in the Pacific. Indeed, one hour after

Japanese air squadrons had commenced bombing in ~~Hawaii and the Philippines~~ *Oahu*

the Japanese Ambassador to the United States and his colleague delivered

to the Secretary of State a formal reply to a ~~former~~ *recent American* message, ~~from the~~

~~Secretary.~~ *While* This reply ~~contained a statement~~ *stated* that diplomatic negotiations

~~must be considered at an end,~~ *it* contained no threat ~~and no~~ *or* hint of ~~an~~ *war or*

armed attack.

It will be recorded that the distance ~~of Manila, and especially~~ of

Hawaii from Japan makes it obvious that the attack ~~were~~ *was* deliberately

planned many days *or even weeks* ago. During the intervening time the Japanese Govern-

ment has deliberately sought to deceive the United States by false

statements and expressions of hope for continued peace.

The attack yesterday on ~~Manila and on the Island of Oahu have~~ *the Hawaiian Islands* *has*

caused severe damage to American naval and military forces. Very

many American lives have been lost. In addition American ~~~~ ships

have been torpodoed on the high seas between San Francisco and

Honolulu.

Yesterday the Japanese Government also launched an attack

against Malaya.

Last night Japanese forces attacked Guam.

Japan has," therefore," undertaken a "surprise offensive extending *The Philippine Islands*

throughout the Pacific area. The facts of yesterday speak for

themselves. The people of the United States have already formed

their opinions and well understand the implications ~~these attacks~~

~~bear on~~ the *to very* safety of our nation.

As Commander-in-Chief of the Army and Navy I have ~~of course,~~

directed that all measures be taken for our defense.

Long will we remember the character of the onslaught against

us.

(A) *No matter how long it may take us to overcome this premeditated invasion the American people will in their righteous might win through to absolute victory.*

I speak the will of the Congress and of the people ~~of this~~

~~country~~ when I assert that we will not only defend ourselves to

the uttermost but will see to it that this form of treachery shall

never endanger us again. Hostilities exist. There is no mincing

the fact that our people, our territory and our interests are in

grave danger.

I, therefore, ask that the Congress declare that since the

unprovoked and dastardly attack by Japan on Sunday, December

seventh, a state of war exists between the United Statew and the

Japanese Empire.

                    ✶✶✶✶✶✶✶✶✶✶✶✶✶✶✶✶✶✶✶✶✶✶✶✶✶

God." By the time the president was ready to sleep the speech was written, waiting safely for history.

As FDR gathered information, dispensed orders, and prepared to address a joint session of Congress, a Sunday became *the* Sunday that the American people would remember the rest of their lives. Unlike more recent events such as the plane crashes into the World Trade Center on September 11, 2001, or even the assassination of President John F. Kennedy on November 22, 1963, there was no clear moment when most Americans learned of Pearl Harbor. There was no Internet or television, of course, and most Americans were accustomed to receiving their news from newspapers. Most were not even listening to the radio. They were relaxing—taking drives, playing golf, spending time with their families, eating Sunday dinner—feeling safe that their country was not a combatant in the wars that were raging in Europe and Asia.

At about 2:30 p.m. EST the United Press International (UPI) and the Columbia Broadcasting System (CBS) flashed the news that the Japanese had attacked Pearl Harbor. About the same time, White House correspondents scrambled back to the center of the action. But even so, the news spread faster over the telephone than it did across the media. Relatives called relatives, friends dialed friends, and those relatives and those friends called others as the flow of information cascaded over America.

In Pittsburgh, Pennsylvania, at the Soldiers and Sailors Memorial Hall, the news interrupted an America First Rally. North Dakota senator Gerald P. Nye, a leader in the noninterventionist cause, had just taken the stage to condemn Roosevelt's foreign policy to a crowd of 1,500 people. It took several interruptions before he grasped the truth and importance of a note he had been handed. Finally he told the audience, "I have before me the worst news that I have encountered in the last twenty years." Then he read the message. Later, dejected by the reality of a

ABOVE | Senator Gerald P. Nye was delivering a speech to an America First Rally in Pittsburgh when he learned about the Pearl Harbor attack. He said it was "the worst news that I have encountered in the last twenty years."

war that he believed FDR had promoted, he told another group, "We have been maneuvered into this by the president, but the only thing now is to declare war and to jump into it with everything we have and bring it to a victorious conclusion."

Nye's venom was not shared by most Americans. Rather than blame, they stood behind their president. Outside the White House people had been gathering since the news broke. They pressed against the iron gate in the front, collected on the steps of the old State Department building, and lined the narrow street to the west. "Evening came, and a misty, ragged moon," wrote a Roosevelt biographer. And still the people came, watching the nation's leaders—their faces drawn and serious—come and go. Then someone began to sing, and soon other voices joined in on a song they all knew:

God bless America,
Land that I love,
Stand beside her and guide her
Thru the night with the light from above.

While they gathered and sang, Roosevelt kept a scheduled appointment with journalist Edward R. Murrow. Over beers and sandwiches, the president spoke openly, too tired to guard his words or worry about the consequences. As he shared the damage reports with Murrow, he pounded his fist on the

table. It had been a debacle. American planes had been destroyed "on the ground, by God, on the ground!" It was unfathomable, unexplainable. Even after hours of meetings and reports he still did not know precisely what had happened.

Soon he was too exhausted to continue. Murrow departed, and at 12:30 a.m., FDR left the oval study for his bedroom.

The House Chamber was packed the next day. Senators, Supreme Court justices, cabinet members, and leaders of the armed forces sat in the front rows, with the House of Representatives behind them. Some of the members of the House had brought their

ABOVE | CBS News correspondent Edward R. Murrow spoke with FDR on the night of December 7. The president pounded his fist on a table as he explained that American planes at Pearl Harbor had been destroyed "on the ground."

children with them to witness the historic event. The press gallery was overflowing; spectators inched into every available space. At 12:29 p.m. a voice cut through the low hum of the chamber: "The President of the United States."

Almost as one person, everyone in the chamber was on their feet, applauding their leader. The cheering continued as Roosevelt, his arm tightly gripping the arm of his son James, slowly made his way toward the rostrum. As he moved forward, the cheering grew louder. Rebel yells mixed with the sharp clapping of hands, and tears from many witnesses accompanied the president on his labored march.

Then silence. Roosevelt began to read his speech. "Yesterday, December seventh, 1941—a date which will live in infamy— the United States of America . . ." When he finished almost everyone in the chamber was standing and applauding. Roosevelt had spoken for only six minutes and thirty seconds, but his words echoed throughout the remainder of the war. No presidential address has equaled its impact.

ABOVE | With righteous indignation in his voice, President Roosevelt asks Congress to declare war on Japan. Only one day had passed since he had received the news.

ABOVE | A packed House Chamber listens to the president's war message. Some members of Congress had brought their children to hear the momentous address.

CHAPTER 9
FIGHTING BACK

After Pearl Harbor they decided to make the biggest and best war ever seen," British lieutenant general Frederick Morgan said of his new American allies. Indeed, not even the smoking wreckage off the coast of Hawaii could obscure the fact that a mighty war machine was gearing up for action. The United States' economy, already recovering from a decade of depression, would soon rev into overdrive.

In the week following the attack, thirteen new warships slid into the water, with a fleet of half-built battleships, cruisers, destroyers, and submarines soon to follow. In early January, 1942, President Roosevelt staggered Congress when he commanded industrialists to produce forty-five thousand aircraft, forty-five thousand tanks, and eight million tons of new shipping within a year. "Oh, the production people can do it if they really try," he told advisors who recommended against setting such outrageous goals.

The audacity of the attack confirmed Western stereotypes that the Japanese were irrational and unpredictable, as if a mental disorder had afflicted the entire nation. Rather than cower before the aggressors, the American people clamored for revenge. Angry young men filed into recruitment centers while radios blared such jingoist tunes

LEFT | The American war machine churned out military goods at an unprecedented rate and in unprecedented numbers. Brought into the war by Pearl Harbor, the crew of this M-4 Sherman tank faced a tough road ahead.

149

DECEMBER 7th 1941 — REMEMBER!!

as "Remember Pearl Harbor" and "We're Gonna Have to Slap the Dirty Little Jap." Many Americans resented getting dragged into the fight, and the sacrifices it would incur, but nevertheless anticipated quick retaliatory action from their military.

The War Department relieved Admiral Kimmel and Lieutenant General Short of their commands within two weeks of Pearl Harbor. Yet those swift steps did not mark the beginning of a massive counteroffensive. Although Pearl Harbor rattled the nation, it could not shake American military planners' conviction that Germany should be the primary focus in a two-front war. Japan posed no immediate threat to either the United

States or Great Britain. Roosevelt, despite public pressure to do otherwise, stuck to the plan: prevent Japan from entrenching too deeply in the Pacific while committing the preponderance of American forces to the European theater. Japan's Axis allies made this decision easier when they foolishly declared war on the United States on December 11, 1941. Roosevelt had not asked Congress for a declaration of war against either Germany or Italy. Had he, it is unlikely that Congress would have granted his request.

Pearl Harbor was not just the beginning of the United States' direct participation in World War II. It was also the beginning of an immense, precisely coordinated Japanese offensive against targets around the Pacific. Japan's striking success at Pearl Harbor translated into an overconfident assurance that the country's Western foes were too soft to mount a sustained resistance. Dreams of dominating the Pacific appeared within the Japanese military's grasp. "We Japanese," exhorted one field manual, "heirs to 2,600 years of a glorious past, have now . . . risen in the cause of the peoples of Asia, and embarked upon a noble and solemn undertaking which will change the course of world history."

Hirohito's subordinates saw several obstacles standing between them and their destiny. China remained a persistent strategic problem. Now, intensifying their war efforts, Japan lashed out at the empires of two more great powers: Great Britain and the United States.

ABOVE | Americans focused on Oahu, but Pearl Harbor was part of a larger Japanese assault on targets in the Pacific. Among the other victims was Hong Kong, which was also attacked on December 7.

Prime Minister Winston Churchill had anticipated Japanese offensives against the empire he oversaw. As he studied the maps tacked on the walls of his subterranean headquarters deep beneath the streets of London, he wondered how long his sparse forces could maintain control over Britain's lightly defended possessions in Asia.

Japanese bombers began pummeling Hong Kong just hours after the second wave of planes cleared Pearl Harbor. Infantry units marching south from China soon joined the attack. A combined Indian-Canadian defense force fought a delaying action, blowing bridges and executing strategic retreats in the futile hope that help might arrive from somewhere. Within days of launching their offensive, Japanese units commanded the high ground overlooking the British lines. They cut the city's main water supply before advancing one bloody yard at a time. Major General Christopher Maltby, commander of the garrison, raised the white flag on Christmas Day. "No further military resistance was possible," Maltby reported.

The Japanese had also marched into Malaya, the long peninsula pointing from Southeast Asia toward Australia. Their pilots decimated British air defenses in a matter of hours, clearing the way so infantry

ABOVE | Japanese tanks roll through the British colony of Malaya in early 1942. Japan's quick victory gave it access to the colony's rich reserves of tin and rubber.

units could chew up their opponents on the ground. Fast-moving detachments on bicycles confused the British, who never knew where the next assault was coming from. Outnumbered and panicked, British soldiers fled in large numbers. Discouraged by the mass exodus, Indian and Malayan troops, most of them poorly trained and reluctant to fight for the preservation of colonial rule, vanished into the jungle.

Several weeks into the Malayan invasion, the principal of a British college in Kuala Lumpur flinched at the sound of a nearby explosion. What was that? he wondered. According to legend, one of his students, Lee Kuan Yew, who would one day become the prime minister of Singapore, responded, "That is the end of the British Empire."

Not even Singapore, the island off the Malayan coast hailed as the "Gibraltar of the Pacific," was safe from the Japanese onslaught. The colony was a model of white privilege. Its thirty thousand Europeans, defended by eighty-five thousand soldiers and a daunting British naval presence, ran roughshod over its five million Asian inhabitants. One local phrasebook allowed English speakers to give such essential commands as "put up the tennis net" in Malay.

Explosions began ripping across Singapore two hours before the Pearl Harbor attack opened. No one could locate the official responsible for shutting off the city's streetlights, so the bombers emptied their bays over well-lit targets. Chaos spread as fires burned.

That evening, two of the jewels of Britain's Pacific fleet, *Prince of Wales* and *Repulse*, steamed away from their slips in search of enemy targets around Singapore. Their campaign lasted only two days before Japanese planes sunk both ships off the coast of Malaya. "In all the war, I never received a more direct shock," Churchill later wrote. After tallying up the damage, Churchill's advisor General Sir Alan Brooke wrote in his diary: "It means that from Africa eastwards to America, through the Indian Ocean and the Pacific, we have lost control of the sea."

Britain lost control of Singapore soon after. Churchill's insistence that the colony could withstand a six-month siege proved wildly optimistic. Japanese soldiers under General Tomoyuki Yamashita encountered little resistance when they stomped onto Singaporean shores on February 8, 1942. "I don't think the men want to fight," lamented Australian major general Henry Gordon Bennett. General Sir Archibald Wavell, in charge of the overall defense, appealed to his men's patriotism. "The honor of the British Empire is at stake," he urged. But honor

could not stop bullets, and the garrison surrendered on February 15 to a Japanese force only half its size.

With their colonies of Hong Kong, Malaya, and Singapore lost, and Burma (present-day Myanmar) under assault, British officials implored the Americans to strengthen their efforts in the Pacific. Their Asian empire lay in ruins. Australia might be the next victim. Or it could be India. Perhaps both.

Churchill's pleas didn't exactly fall on deaf ears. Significant elements of the American navy supported a larger presence in the Pacific. Roosevelt nevertheless held his course despite a flood of bad news from Asia. Most of FDR's constituents couldn't find the tiny island of Guam, which was closer to Japan than it was to the United States, on a map. It nevertheless stung when seven hundred troops from Japan's Special Naval Landing Forces steamrolled Guam's American defenders within forty-eight hours of Pearl Harbor. Japan took about five hundred prisoners and began digging into what had been one of the United States' important, if undermanned, Pacific bases.

The carrier *Enterprise* had recently delivered a detachment of marines to reinforce Wake Island, a coral atoll over two thousand

ABOVE | Japanese forces overwhelmed Guam in just three days. Following a harsh period of occupation, the US took back the island in 1944. Surviving Japanese soldiers found themselves interred in POW camps.

miles west of Hawaii. This maneuver kept the ship out of Pearl Harbor on December 7 but did nothing to stem the Japanese tide. Planes began bombing Wake Island a few hours after the Pearl Harbor attack ceased. Explosions ripped across the island even as residents of Hong Kong and Singapore were diving for cover a few thousand miles away.

A detachment from Admiral Nagumo's fleet arrived a few days before Christmas to finish the job. "The scene was too beautiful to be a battlefield," one Japanese journalist wrote while watching shells hammer the island. American marines mounted a valiant resistance, killing more than 800 enemy soldiers while losing 120 of their own. It wasn't enough. After a few days of brutal fighting, a sergeant waved a mop handle with a white rag attached to it. Wake Island became one

more piece of the swelling Japanese empire.

Panicked by a string of defeats, American officials anticipated a ground invasion of Hawaii at any moment. In Japan, too, officers were discussing the merits of occupying the islands. Capturing Hawaii would both prevent the Americans from repairing its wounded Pearl Harbor fleet and shove them all the way back to California. On the other hand, Hawaii was so far from Japan that it would be difficult to supply and even more difficult to defend. Moreover, a Hawaiian offensive would consume forces intended for the conquest of Southeast Asia, which remained Japan's top priority. Ultimately, Japanese military leaders decided against an invasion.

Admiral Nagumo's First Air Fleet completed its mission when it reached port on

ABOVE | F4F-3 Wildcats destroyed during the Japanese assault on Wake Island. The American garrison, which numbered in the hundreds, had no chance against a superior Japanese force.

ABOVE | American air crews write messages to their Japanese targets. Japan's inability to keep up with American military production factored into its decision to launch a surprise attack.

December 23, the same day Wake Island fell. A smiling Admiral Yamamoto boarded *Akagi* the next morning to greet the conquerors who had brought his daring plan to fruition. "You men trained hard and patiently, and your operation against Pearl Harbor was a great success," he said. "You must remember," he warned, "that in spite of this important victory, we have only entered upon the first stage of this war and we have only completed one operation. . . . There are many more battles ahead."

Flashbulbs snapped as the sailors cheered, their voices ringing far and wide across Hiroshima Bay.

For the Japanese, the next stage of the war had already begun. On December 22, more than forty thousand soldiers under the command of Lieutenant General Masaharu Homma marched ashore from Lingayen Gulf in Luzon, the largest of the Philippine Islands. Even though many American officials had expected the Philippines to bear the brunt of the initial Japanese offensive—a blow that instead landed at Pearl Harbor—the commanding officer of its defense forces, General Douglas MacArthur, showed a curious passivity when he

ABOVE | General MacArthur promised to return to the Philippines. When the Americans did, in 1944, they faced stiff resistance that lasted for nearly a year.

received word that the war had started. Within hours of the first torpedo strikes in Hawaii, MacArthur's subordinates were urging him to unleash his B-17 bombers on Japanese-occupied Taiwan, a few hundred miles to the north. Instead he did nothing, failing even to scatter his planes around the airfield. Soon, a swarm of Japanese fighters and bombers appeared on the horizon and swiftly obliterated MacArthur's tightly packed aircraft, establishing air superiority in the Philippines before President Roosevelt had even declared war.

When General Homma launched his attack, MacArthur reluctantly withdrew his combined American-Filipino forces to the Bataan Peninsula in the southwest corner of Luzon. MacArthur moved himself, his family, and his staff to the nearby island fortress of Corregidor. Never shy about publicity, the general issued bombastic statements promising to "[deny] the foe the sacred soil of the Philippines."

In reality, the 110,000 soldiers and civilians at Bataan were in serious trouble. They lacked adequate stockpiles of food and medicine. Starving, and suffering from malaria and other tropical diseases, MacArthur's men absorbed attack after attack. The enemy was in bad shape too, frustrated by their stalled

ABOVE | American prisoners carry their exhausted comrades in improvised stretchers. Thousands died before completing the sixty-five-mile death march from Bataan, in the Philippines, to a prison camp.

offensive and reeling from the same diseases that plagued the defenders of Bataan.

MacArthur sent his men a steady stream of assurances that help was on the way. He was wrong. The War Department knew the Philippine Islands were indefensible. Devoting scarce resources to lifting the siege would be folly. "There are times when men have to die," Secretary of War Stimson recorded in his diary.

Roosevelt ordered MacArthur to abandon Corregidor for Australia. The general was more valuable as a symbol of American resolve than as a statistic on a casualty roll. MacArthur, along with his wife, his son, and seventeen members of his staff, boarded a PT boat on March 12 for a nighttime race to

safety. "I shall return," he declared on reaching South Australia's Adelaide train station.

The defenders of Bataan surrendered on April 9. "Will our troops be well treated?" Major General Edward King asked. "We are not barbarians," his captors replied.

Corregidor fell around a month later. With it went the last hopes of the United States retaining control of the Philippines. Its defenders put up a determined fight but finally broke under weeks of bombing, starvation, illness, and living in dank tunnels carved into the island. General Jonathan Wainwright, who led the inspiring if hopeless resistance, radioed a final message to Washington: "With profound regret and with continued pride in my gallant troops I go to meet the Japanese commander. . . . Good-bye, Mr. President."

Wainwright became one of the roughly seventy thousand prisoners of war taken in the Philippines. The Japanese had anticipated capturing around half that number. With their own supplies stretched thin and a lifetime of lessons about the inferiority of outsiders in their heads, they treated their prisoners with a brutality born from a combination of necessity and racism. Filipino captives became targets for bayonet practice. Sick captives were left behind to die, and starving ones were buried alive.

ABOVE | Lieutenant General Jonathan Wainwright led a spirited defense at Bataan. "If the Japanese can take the Rock," he said, "they'll find me here." He was taken prisoner and survived the war.

Regrettably, similar situations occurred throughout the vast Japanese empire. Occupied forces brutalized Chinese populations, raped and murdered their way across Hong Kong, and conducted mass executions in Singapore.

"DOOLITTLE DOOD IT" screamed a headline from the May 19, 1942 edition of the *Los Angeles Herald Express*. This unusual proclamation celebrated an unusual operation that in a small way mirrored the assault on Pearl Harbor while opening a new phase of the Pacific War.

Ever since December 7, President Roosevelt had urged the War Department to find a way to hit targets inside Japan. FDR knew the military could not inflict much physical damage, but it could reverse the psychology of the conflict, giving Americans reason for hope while putting Japan on notice that harsh consequences awaited them.

The task fell to Lieutenant Colonel James H. Doolittle, a former test pilot who held both air-speed records and a doctorate in aeronautical engineering. His force of

ABOVE | Major General Jimmy Doolittle (fifth from left) and his crew in China after completing the morale-lifting raid on Tokyo.

sixteen B-25 bombers accepted a mission so foolhardy it was almost impudent. After taking off from the carrier *Hornet*, Doolittle would lead his squadron in a raid on Tokyo, then, once they ran out of fuel, crash-land in China and hope for the best. Fearing leaks, no one informed Chiang Kai-shek's government that the Americans were coming until the last possible moment.

Doolittle's men spent a month practicing takeoffs and refining the details of their one-way ride. Like the Japanese preparing for Pearl Harbor, they studied their targets— factories, mills, public utilities—with single-minded intensity. In early April, *Hornet* left San Francisco for its rendezvous with the carrier *Enterprise* in the North Pacific. From there, "Task Force Mike" punched through wicked storms toward Japan.

A Japanese patrol boat stumbled across the fleet when it was still seven hundred miles from Doolittle's objective. American cruisers

ABOVE | The carrier *Hornet* was in the Atlantic on December 7. It was then transferred to the Pacific, where it carried Doolittle's planes and later participated in the Battle of Midway and other campaigns.

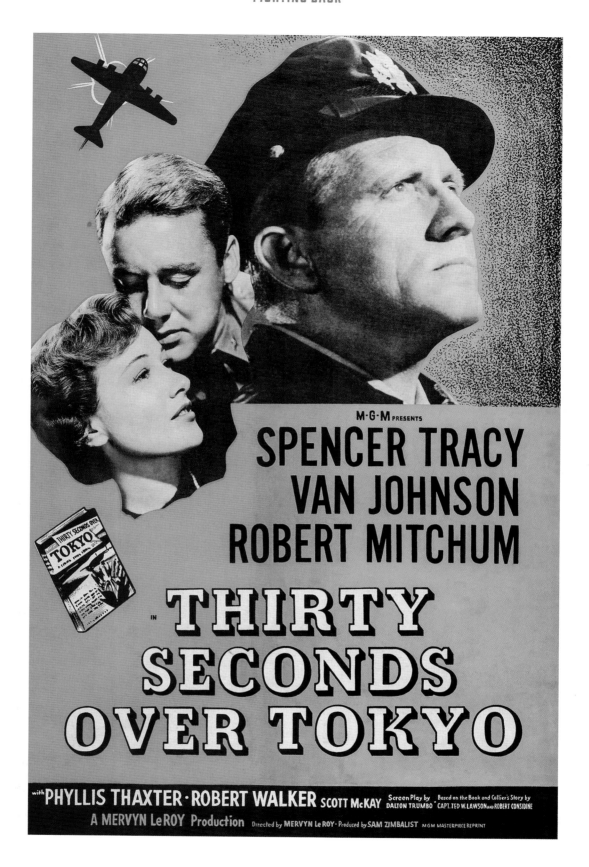

ABOVE | Based on a 1943 book of the same name, *Thirty Seconds over Tokyo* (1944) used Hollywood stars to bring the story of the Doolittle Raid to a mass audience.

quickly sunk the ship, but the encounter forced the planes to launch earlier than anticipated, reducing their odds of reaching China safely.

"Good luck and God bless you," Admiral Bull Halsey radioed just before the first overloaded B-25 wobbled off *Hornet*'s deck at 8:20 a.m. on April 18. "I don't want to set the world on fire, just Tokyo" read a message chalked on to one of the bombs stowed aboard a plane. Slipping into formation behind Doolittle, the B-25s winged their way toward an unsuspecting Japan. Thirteen of them, including Doolittle's, headed for Tokyo. Others peeled off toward Kobe, Nagoya, and Osaka. One landed at Vladivostok, Russia, after experiencing fuel problems. The Soviets held the plane and its crew for more than a year.

By no means was it a suicide mission, but the Americans knew there was a good chance they would never see their loved ones again. Doolittle informed his men that, should his plane get hit, he was going to "dive in, full throttle, into any target I can find where the crash will do the most good."

Tokyo Bay came into view two hours after takeoff. The B-25s sped across the water, unhindered by barrage balloons, which had been lowered following an air-raid drill that morning. As at Pearl Harbor, many residents mistook the incoming planes for friendlies, waving at what they assumed were Japanese pilots.

Explosions from the first bombs convinced the Japanese that the impossible was happening: their islands were under attack. After striking several targets, Doolittle's raiders raced away before the Japanese mounted any serious resistance. Only one of the B-25s suffered any damage—a few nicks from anti-aircraft fire.

The attackers flew toward China, their fuel reserves dipping lower and lower. Finally, their tanks empty, they slid one by one toward the ground. "It was as if some great hand had reached down through the storm, seized the plane and crunched it in a closing fist," remembered Lieutenant Ted Lawson of the moment of impact. "Then nothing," he continued. "Nothing but peace. A strange, strange peaceful feeling. There wasn't any pain. A great, restful quiet surrounded me."

Chinese guerrillas spirited most of the raiders to safety. Three Americans died in a plane crash. Japanese soldiers captured eight others, executing three of them. Japan also retaliated by launching a murderous campaign in China that ultimately left around 250,000 people dead.

Despite these losses, which Americans did not learn of until much later, the United

ABOVE | Japan's empire expanded greatly in the first half of 1942. With carriers like *Yorktown* (above) bolstering the fleet, the United States scored its first major victory in the June 1942 Battle of Midway.

States celebrated its revenge for Pearl Harbor. "Here is America's answer to treachery," one newsreel narrator enthused a few weeks after the attack. Doolittle's raid had only negligible impact on the Japanese war machine yet left its military hierarchy profoundly shaken. "The Japanese people had been told they were invulnerable," Doolittle wrote, so the attack created doubts about "the reliability of their leaders."

The Japanese government wanted to ensure that American carriers could never again get close enough to launch a surprise attack. Two days after Doolittle's raid, Japan's military leaders scrutinized another of Admiral Yamamoto's bold plans. The architect of Pearl Harbor proposed attacking Midway Island, an American possession in the Central Pacific. Capturing that outpost would protect the Japanese homeland while pushing the enemy farther back.

Yamamoto's detractors argued that taking Midway would stretch their forces too thin while diverting their focus from Southeast Asia. But with Tokyo residents feeling jittery and a desire for reprisal pervading

ABOVE | Midway confirmed what some strategists believed even before Pearl Harbor: the age of the battleship had passed. Naval air power, such as the American planes striking the Japanese carrier *Hiryu*, shown above, was now the king of the sea.

the room, the Imperial General Staff, with Admiral Nagumo's support, green-lighted the Midway campaign.

"I can guarantee to put up a tough fight for the first six months," Yamamoto replied when asked in 1940 about the prospect of war with the United States, "but I have absolutely no confidence as to what would happen if it went on for two or three years." He began planning the conquest of Midway, never suspecting that an American carrier that had escaped destruction at Pearl Harbor—*Enterprise*—along with two other carriers, *Hornet* and *Yorktown*, would be waiting for them, ready to deliver the blow that turned the tide of the war that began on that picture-perfect December morning. At the Battle of Midway, the American fleet sent four of the carriers involved in the Pearl Harbor offensive to the ocean floor: *Akagi*, *Hiryu*, *Kaga*, and *Soryu*. The United States wrapped up its victory in the Battle of Midway on June 7, 1942, exactly six months after the date which will live in infamy.

ABOVE | American planes sank Japan's heavy cruiser *Mikuma*, shown above, at Midway, along with four of its aircraft carriers. The Japanese navy never really recovered from the United States' surprise offensive.

EPILOGUE
A PART OF WHO YOU ARE

Pearl Harbor never dies, and no living person has seen the end of it," Lieutenant Edward F. Hanify wrote Admiral Kimmel in 1953. Hanify was right. The attack on Pearl Harbor has been dissected countless times in the decades since that fateful December morning, as have the labyrinth of decisions, misunderstandings, and oversights that enabled the Japanese to catch the American fleet by surprise. Even as the World War II generation dwindles in numbers, Pearl Harbor retains its symbolic power. Since 1941 various factions have used it to unify the United States, advance political agendas, and warn Americans that they must never again be caught unprepared.

Occurring before the rise of video cameras and smartphones, the attack remained a largely imagined event in the minds of World War II–era Americans. People could read about it or view still images of it, including some of the ones presented in this book, but precious little motion picture footage of the event came out of Hawaii.

Hollywood, newly mobilized behind the war effort, stepped in to fill the gap. Motion pictures made during the war argued that Japanese treachery had inadvertently unified the

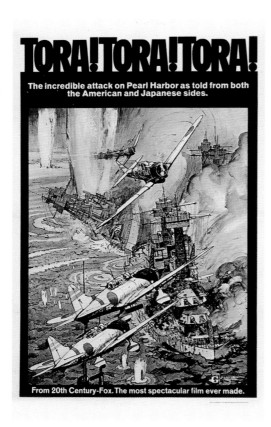

TORA! TORA! TORA!

The incredible attack on Pearl Harbor as told from both the American and Japanese sides.

From 20th Century-Fox. The most spectacular film ever made.

normally peaceful American people behind the idea of war. The docudrama *December 7th* (1943), often credited to John Ford but actually the work of Ford, cinematographer Gregg Toland, and many others, recreated the attack so convincingly that many subsequent films, such as Frank Capra's *Prelude to War*, have represented clips from it as the genuine article.

Replete with stirring shots of battle damage, *December 7th*'s climax preaches a message of national unity. "This war is a war of survival, a people's war," a narrator intones over scenes of schoolchildren trying on gas masks and participating in defense drills. As patriotic music plays, loyal Japanese Americans living in Hawaii close their language schools and paint over Japanese-language signs. One restaurant owner exchanges a "Bonzai Café" sign for one reading "Keep 'em Flying Café." The film closes with a verbal shot across Prime Minister Tojo's bow. "To all this treachery there can be but one answer," the narrator warns, "a time-honored answer: For all they that take the sword, shall perish with the sword."

The attack has been a subject of interest for generations of filmmakers. It served as background context for the memorable *From Here to Eternity* (1953), starring Burt Lancaster, Montgomery Clift, and Deborah Kerr. It took center stage in 1970's *Tora! Tora! Tora!*, which symbolized the new cooperation between the United States and Japan by using an international cast and crew to tell the Pearl Harbor story from both sides' perspectives. The Ben Affleck vehicle *Pearl Harbor* (2001) found little critical favor but nevertheless introduced the attack to younger audiences while touching off a renewed flurry of interest in World War II.

Whereas moviemakers such as John Ford brought people together, inquiries into what "really" happened at Pearl Harbor have often created divisions and controversy. It

ABOVE | With its international crew and multiple perspectives, the 1970 film *Tora! Tora! Tora!* symbolized the increasing closeness between the United States and Japan. Even so, many critics panned the movie as preachy and dull.

wasn't long before anti-Roosevelt newspapers and Republicans started asking whether the president bore at least partial blame for the attack. Perhaps, some suggested, Roosevelt might even have known about Japan's plans but said nothing because he was looking for a way into the conflict. While never proven and repeatedly discredited, this "back door to war" theory has spawned whole shelves of books and fueled debates raging in various corners of the Internet.

A series of official investigations have blamed various parties for failing to adequately prepare for an attack. These panels have provided historians with a massive amount of primary-source information in the form of interviews and sworn testimony from eyewitnesses. Convened at FDR's request within days of the attack, the Roberts Commission, named after its chair, Supreme Court Justice Owen J. Roberts, charged both Admiral Kimmel and Lieutenant General Short with dereliction of duty while largely exonerating the Roosevelt administration and the top brass in Washington. Twin investigations conducted by the army and navy in 1944 softened the blow when they accused Kimmel and Short of errors of judgment rather than dereliction of duty. At the same time, the army shifted blame upwards, arguing that General Marshall failed to adequately inform his subordinates about

ABOVE | Hollywood kept returning to the Day of Infamy. *Pearl Harbor* (2001) was a big-budget, action-packed, effects-laden spectacle that introduced a new generation to the attack.

Japan's activities. Another navy inquiry, this one conducted in 1945 under Vice Admiral H. Kent Hewitt, produced more pages of documentary evidence while essentially supporting the conclusions of previous probes.

Throughout the war years Republican congressmen demanded additional investigations. The Democratic majority squelched this demand both out of concern for national security (no one wanted the Japanese to know about Magic, for example) and from fear of the political damage congressional hearings might incur. The Democrats finally conceded in 1946, when Senate Majority Leader and future Vice President Alben Barkley created the Joint Committee on the Investigation of the Pearl Harbor Attack. Newspapers offered breathless coverage as Kimmel, Short, and Stark all testified in hopes of clearing their names. Following months of hearings, the committee's report rejected the "back door to war" theory, confirmed the "errors in judgment" evaluation of previous boards, and concluded that officials in both Washington and Hawaii were guilty of poor communication.

These investigations produced reams of material establishing exactly what had happened, and why. But the past is never past, of course. Campaigns to restore the reputations of Kimmel and others stretched into

the early twenty-first century. While in some cases arising from a sincere desire to clear officers of blame, some of these efforts were designed at least in part to discredit the Roosevelt administration, which remains a guiding star for political liberals.

On a broader scale, "Pearl Harbor" still serves as a convenient shorthand for anyone who sees a potential threat to Americans' national security. Throughout the Cold War with the Soviet Union, for example, politicians and editorialists issued a constant stream of warnings that the communists might launch a nuclear Pearl Harbor against an unsuspecting United States. Constant vigilance was the eternal watchword.

For most modern-day Americans, their day of infamy came on September 11, 2001. "The Pearl Harbor of the twenty-first century took place today," President George W. Bush wrote in his diary just a few hours after the Twin Towers collapsed. "Infamy!" screamed headlines across the nation. Once again, accusations flew as people from across the political spectrum sought to assign blame for a surprise attack.

None of these echoes of Pearl Harbor—neither the cinematic spectacles, nor the bestselling books, nor the splashy headlines inspired by the latest probe into the facts of the attack—really offer the best way of

remembering what happened on December 7, 1941. For that, one must travel to Hawaii, where the rusted hulk of *Arizona* lies on the ocean floor just off the coast of Oahu. A sweeping, white memorial, opened in 1962, transects the wreck, which holds the remains of 1,102 American sailors. From this vantage point one can appreciate both the staggering beauty of Pearl Harbor and the horrors that visited it all those years ago. The memorial signifies not only the sacrifices made in wartime, but also the conviction that those sacrifices helped create a more peaceful world.

On December 7, 1991, President George H. W. Bush offered his thoughts on Pearl Harbor's meaning for a society rapidly emerging from a half-century-long Cold War. With the *Arizona* monument swooping behind him like a ramp to the heavens, he told the thousands gathered to mark the fiftieth anniversary of the attack that "I have no rancor in my heart toward Germany or Japan." Recognizing that former enemies were now staunch allies, he observed that "the values we hold dear as a nation—equality of opportunity, freedom of religion and

ABOVE | The meaning and relevance of Pearl Harbor evolves along with world events. On September 11, 2001, the nation turned to history to find words to explain another surprise attack on American soil.

speech and assembly, free and vigorous elections—are now revered by many nations. Our greatest victory in World War II took place not on the field of battle, but in the nations we once counted as foes."

President Bush, a former naval aviator who in 1989 attended Emperor Hirohito's funeral, recognized that he could never truly

escape that beautiful, horrifying Sunday morning fifty years before. "As you look back on life and retrace the steps that made you the person you are, you pick out the turning points, the defining moments," he told his fellow World War II veterans. "Pearl Harbor defines a part of who you are."

ABOVE | The USS *Arizona* memorial in Pearl Harbor is a poignant and beautiful monument.

ABOUT THE AUTHORS

Randy Roberts is Distinguished Professor of History at Purdue University. His most recent book, coauthored with Johnny Smith, is *Blood Brothers: The Fatal Friendship Between Muhammad Ali and Malcolm X.* Among his other books are *Jack Dempsey: The Manassa Mauler* (1979); *Papa Jack: Jack Johnson and the Era of White Hopes* (1983); *"But They Can't Beat Us": Oscar Robertson and the Crispus Attucks Tigers* (1999); *Joe Louis: Hard Times Man* (2010); *A Team for America: The Army-Navy Game That Rallied a Nation* (2011); with Ed Krzemienski, *Rising Tide: Bear Bryant, Joe Namath, and Dixie's Last Quarter* (2013); and, with James S. Olson, *John Wayne American* (1995), *A Line in the Sand: The Alamo in Blood and Memory* (2000), *Winning Is the Only Thing: Sports in America since 1945* (1989), and *Where the Domino Fell: America and Vietnam, 1945–1990* (1989). Roberts has served frequently as a consultant and on-camera commentator for PBS, HBO, and the History Channel. He lives in Lafayette, Indiana, with his wife, Marjie.

David Welky is a professor of history at the University of Central Arkansas. A specialist in twentieth-century American history, he is the author of *A Wretched and Precarious Situation: In Search of the Last Arctic Frontier* (2016), *Marching Across the Color Line: A. Philip Randolph and Civil Rights in the World War II Era* (2013), *The Thousand-Year Flood: The Ohio-Mississippi Disaster of 1937* (2011), *The Moguls and the Dictators: Hollywood and the Coming of World War II* (2008), and other books. He lives in Conway, Arkansas, with his wife and two children.

IMAGE CREDITS

Front cover: Farm Security Administration - Office of War Information Photograph Collection (LOC)

Page 2: top left: ©Universal History Archive / UIG / Bridgeman Images; top right: Courtesy of NARA; middle right: © INTERFOTO / Alamy Stock Photo; middle left: US Government Printing Office #1943 542951 / University of North Texas; lower right: Courtesy of NARA; bottom left: Courtesy of NARA; bottom right: Courtesy of the US Air Force

Page 6: ©Aviation History Collection / Alamy Stock Photo

Page 8: Courtesy of LOC

Page 10: ©Pictures from History / Bridgeman Images

Page 12: Courtesy of the National Diet Library, Tokyo, Japan

Page 13: ©Private Collection / Peter Newark Pictures / Bridgeman Images

Page 14: ©SZ Photo / Scherl / Bridgeman Images

Page 15: ©Pictures from History / Bridgeman Images

Page 16: public domain under US copyright law

Page 17: ©Look and Learn / Bridgeman Images

Page 18: ©Private Collection / Peter Newark Military Pictures / Bridgeman Images

Page 19: ©Pictures from History / Bridgeman Images

Page 20: ©Pictures from History / Bridgeman Images

Page 21: China Incident Photograph Album, Volume 2

Page 22: ©Pictures from History / Bridgeman Images

Page 23: ©EPA european pressphoto agency b.v./ Alamy Stock Photo

Page 25: Courtesy of NARA

Page 26: Courtesy of Everett Collection

Page 28: ©Private Collection / Peter Newark American Pictures/Bridgeman Images

Page 30: Courtesy of NHHC

Page 31: ©Pictures from History / Bridgeman Images

Page 32: Courtesy of Everett Collection

Page 33: ©Private Collection / Peter Newark Military Pictures/Bridgeman Images

Page 34: Courtesy of Everett Collection

Page 35: Courtesy of Everett Collection

Page 36: ©John Frost Newspapers / Alamy Stock Photo

Page 37: Advertising Archive / Everett Collection

Page 38: By Partridge, Rondal, 1917–2015, Photographer (NARA record: 8464464)

Page 39: top: Courtesy Everett Collection; bottom: ©Mirrorpix/Bridgeman Images

Page 40: Courtesy of Everett Collection

Page 41: Courtesy of Everett Collection

Page 42: Courtesy of Everett Collection

Page 43: ©DILTZ / Bridgeman Images

Page 44: Courtesy of Everett Collection

Page 45: Courtesy of Everett Collection

Page 46: ©Pictures from History/Bridgeman Images

Page 48: From the George Grantham Bain: Collection - LOC

Page 49: ©Private Collection / The Stapleton: Collection/Bridgeman Images

Page 51: ©De Agostini Picture Library / Bridgeman: Images

Page 52: ©Fleet Admiral Isoruku Yamamoto (colour litho), Japanese School, (20th century) / Private Collection / Peter Newark Military Pictures / Bridgeman Images

Page 53: Courtesy of NARA

Page 54: ©WorldPhotos / Alamy Stock Photo

Page 55: Courtesy of LOC

Page 56: Courtesy of NHHC

Page 57: public domain under Japanese copyright law

Page 59: ©Private Collection / Peter Newark Military Pictures / Bridgeman Images

Page 60: ©Universal History Archive / UIG / Bridgeman Images

Page 61: ©Lebrecht Music and Arts Photo Library / Alamy Stock Photo

Page 62: ©NHHC

Page 63: ©World History Archive / Alamy Stock Photo

Page 64: ©Pictures from History / Bridgeman Images

Page 66: ©Sueddeutsche Zeitung Photo / Alamy Stock Photo

Page 67: ©robert cicchetti / Alamy Stock Photo

Page 68: Courtesy of NHHC

Page 69: Courtesy of Everett Collection

Page 70: UIG / Courtesy Everett Collection

Page 71: Underwood Archives / UIG / Bridgeman Images

Page 72: ©Sueddeutsche Zeitung Photo / Alamy Stock Photo

Page 73: top: public domain under US copyright law; bottom: public domain under Japanese copyright law

Page 74: Courtesy of NARA

Page 75: ©Chiang Kai-shek (1887–1975), Chinese political and military leader (Kuomintang) here c. 1940 / Bridgeman Images

Page 77: Courtesy of NARA

Page 79: Courtesy of the Department of Defense / University of North Texas

Page 80: From Shizuo Fukui - Kure Maritime Museum, Japanese Naval Warship Photo Album

Page 82: Mirrorpix / Courtesy of Everett Collection

Page 83: public domain under Japanese copyright law

Page 84: Courtesy of NHHC

Page 85: public domain under Japanese copyright law

Page 86: Courtesy of NMUSN

Page 87: Courtesy of NARA

Page 88: ©Everett Collection Historical / Alamy Stock Photo

Page 90: Courtesy of NHHC

Page 91: Courtesy of the United States Army

Page 92: Courtesy of NARA

Page 93: Courtesy of NMUSN

Page 95: ©Pictures from History / Bridgeman Images

Page 96: Courtesy of NHHC

Page 98: Courtesy of NASA

Page 100: Courtesy of NARA

Page 101: ©Private Collection / Peter Newark Military Pictures / Bridgeman Images

Page 103: Courtesy of NARA

Page 104: Courtesy of NARA

Page 105: Courtesy of NMUSN

Page 107: Courtesy of NARA

Page 108: Courtesy of NHHC

Page 109: Courtesy of LOC

Page 110: Courtesy of NARA

Page 111: Courtesy of NARA

Page 112: Farm Security Administration - Office of War Information Photograph Collection (LOC)

Page 114: Courtesy of NARA

Page 115: Courtesy of NHHC

Page 116: Courtesy of NHHC

Page 117: Courtesy of NARA

Page 118: Courtesy of the US Navy Art Gallery

Page 119: top: Courtesy of NARA; bottom left: Courtesy NHHC; bottom right: Courtesy of NARA

Page 120–121: Commander Griffith Bailey Coale, USNR, Official US Navy Combat Artist, 1944; Courtesy of the US Navy Art Center, Washington, DC Official US Navy Photograph, now in the collections of the National Archives.

Page 122: Courtesy of NARA

Page 123: Taken by Hajime Yoshida, public domain under Japanese copyright law

Page 125: Courtesy of NARA

Page 127: UIG / Everett Collection

Page 128: Department of Defense. Department of the Navy, Naval Photographic Center

Page 129: Courtesy of the US Air Force

Page 130: Courtesy of Everett Collection

Page 132: Courtesy of NARA

Page 133: Courtesy of NMUSN

Page 135: From the Harris & Ewing Collection / LOC

Page 136: Courtesy of NARA, Office of Presidential Libraries. Harry S. Truman Library

Page 137: Executive Office of the President of the United States

Page 138: ©General George C. Marshall, 1941 (b/w photo), German Photographer (20th century)/© SZ Photo / Bridgeman Images

Page 139: Courtesy of NARA

Page 140: Courtesy of Everett Collection

Page 141–143: Papers as President, Master Speech File; Franklin D. Roosevelt Library (NLFDR); NARA.

Page 144: Courtesy of LOC

Page 145: Courtesy of Everett Collection

Page 146: © Pictorial Press Ltd / Alamy Stock Photo

Page 147: ©INTERFOTO / Alamy Stock Photo

Page 148: Courtesy of LOC

Page 150: Charles Alston / NARA

Page 151: Courtesy of NARA

Page 152: ©PVDE / Bridgeman Images

Page 153: Mondadori / Everett Collection

Page 155: Courtesy of Everett Collection

Page 156: Courtesy of NARA

Page 157: Courtesy of NARA

Page 158: ©INTERFOTO / Alamy Stock Photo

Page 159: Courtesy of NARA

Page 160: Courtesy of NARA

Page 161: UIG \ Everett Collection

Page 162: Courtesy of the National Museum of the Air Force

Page 163: Courtesy of Everett Collection

Page 165: Courtesy of NHHC

Page 166: Courtesy of NARA

Page 167: Courtesy of NARA

Page 168: Courtesy of the Office for Emergency Management. Office of War Information. Domestic Operations Branch. Bureau of Graphics

Page 170: Courtesy of Everett Collection

Page 171: ©AF archive / Alamy Stock Photo

Page 173: ©culliganphoto / Alamy Stock Photo

Page 174: ©US Navy Photo / Alamy Stock Photo

....

LOC: The Library of Congress, Prints and Photographs Division, Washington, DC

NARA: The National Archives and Records Administration

NASA: The National Aeronautics and Space Administration

NHHC: Naval History and Heritage Command; http://www.history.navy.mil

NMUSN: The National Museum of the US Navy, Washington Navy Yard, Washington, DC